SAGE RESEARCH PROGRESS SERIES IN CRIMINOLOGY
VOLUME 13

STRUCTURE, LAW, and POWER

Essays in the Sociology of Law

Edited by PAUL J. BRANTINGHAM
and JACK M. KRESS

Published in cooperation with the
AMERICAN SOCIETY of CRIMINOLOGY

SAGE Publications   Beverly Hills   London

For information address:

SAGE Publications, Inc.
275 South Beverly Drive
Beverly Hills, California 90212

SAGE PUBLICATIONS, Ltd.
28 Banner Street
London EC1Y 8QE, England

Printed in the United States of America

Library of Congress Cataloging in Publication Data
Main entry under title:

Structure, law, and power.

(Sage research progress series in criminology; v. 13)
   Selected papers presented at the 30th annual meeting of the American Society of Criminology, held in Dallas, Nov. 8-12, 1978.
   Bibliography: p.
   1. Criminal law—Congresses. 2. Sociological jurisprudence—Congresses. 3. Criminal law—United States—Congresses. 4. Criminal law—Canada—Congresses, 5. Crime and criminals—Congresses. I. Brantingham, Paul J. II. Kress, Jack M. III. American Society of Criminology. IV. Series.
K5029.S78   340.1'15   79-18127

ISBN 0-8039-1318-4
ISBN 0-8039-1319-2 pbk.

FIRST PRINTING

K
5029
.S78

CONTENTS

441130

ABOUT THE SERIES

The SAGE RESEARCH PROGRESS SERIES IN CRIMINOLOGY is intended for those professionals and students in the fields of criminology, criminal justice, and law who are interested in the nature of current research in their fields. Each volume in the series—four to six new titles will be published in each calendar year—focuses on a theme of current and enduring concern; and each volume contains a selection of previously unpublished essays . . . drawing on presentations made at the previous year's Annual Meeting of the American Society of Criminology.

Now in its third year, the series continues with five new volumes, composed of papers presented at the 30th Annual Meeting of the American Society of Criminology, held in Dallas, Texas, November 8-12, 1978. The volumes in the third year of publication include:

- *Biology and Crime*
  edited by C. R. Jeffery
- *Perspectives on Victimology*
  edited by William H. Parsonage
- *Police Work: Strategies and Outcomes in Law Enforcement*
  edited by David M. Petersen
- *Structure, Law, and Power: Essays in the Sociology of Law*
  edited by Paul J. Brantingham and Jack M. Kress
- *Courts and Diversion: Policy and Operations Studies*
  edited by Patricia L. Brantingham and Thomas G. Blomberg

Previously published volumes include *Violent Crime: Historical and Contemporary Issues* (James A. Inciardi and Anne E. Pottieger, eds.), *Law and Sanctions: Theoretical Perspectives* (Marvin D. Krohn and Ronald L. Akers, eds.), *The Evolution of Criminal Justice: A Guide for Practical Criminologists* (John P. Conrad, ed.), *Quantitative Studies in Criminology* (Charles Wellford, ed.), *Discretion and Control* (Margaret Evans, ed.), *Theory in Criminology: Contemporary Views* (Robert F. Meier, ed.), *Juvenile Delinquency: Little Brother Grows Up* (Theodore N. Ferdinand, ed.), *Contemporary Corrections: Social Control and Conflict* (C. Ronald Huff, ed.), and *Criminal Justice Planning and Development* (Alvin W. Cohn, ed.). Comments and suggestions from our readers about this series are welcome.

SERIES EDITORS:

James A. Inciardi
University of Delaware

C. Ray Jeffery
Florida State University

Paul J. Brantingham
Simon Fraser University
Jack M. Kress
State University of New York at Albany

INTRODUCTION

In selecting these essays on the sociology of criminal law, we have been guided by a conceptual framework akin to what Nonet (1976) has lately called *jurisprudential sociology*. We generally believe that a proper understanding of the relationship of law and criminology requires an explanation of their symbiotic origins, substance, structure, usage, and metamorphosis over time. We also believe that the development of such understanding and explanation requires a merger of the perspectives, methods, and findings of lawyers, jurists, philosophers, sociologists, and political scientists (at a minimum), and that any emerging science of criminal law is most likely to develop untidily—sometimes rationally, sometimes inductively—but with careful attention both to issues of value and to empirical data.

The criminology of the past 15 years represents a major departure from the North American criminology of the prior half century. Edwin Sutherland summarized that past when he observed that sociology of law was one of the three principal divisions of criminology, but that it was seldom included in general books on the subject (1947: 1). Karl Llewellyn, the legal realist, gave voice to lawyers' frustrations with criminologists when he protested against "smuggish assertions among my sociological friends, such as: 'I take the sociological, *not* the legal, approach to crime' . . . though it is surely obvious that when you take 'the legal' out you also take out 'crime.' " (1962: 353). Sutherland's criminology text (1947), like Mannheim's two-volume criminology treatise (1965), was free of any burden of sociology of law.

During the 1960s criminology changed; sociology of criminal law became a major component of the field. A variety of important anthologies have appeared (e.g., Quinney, 1969; Akers and Hawkins, 1975) as well as texts (e.g., Chambliss and Seidmann, 1971) and a large number of significant monographs (e.g., Platt, 1969; Lemert, 1970; Thompson, 1975; Black, 1976; Berk et al., 1977). Most criminology texts now have significant sociology of law components (e.g., Reid, 1979; Sykes, 1978; Nettler, 1978; and compare with Sutherland and Cressey, 1970: vi).

The extant literature on sociology of criminal law, however, tends to fall into two general classes: the narrowly empirical—concerned primarily with testing propositions derived from the work of sociologists to the exclusion of other social scientists, philosophers, lawyers, or practitioners—and the polemical, concerned primarily with winning ideological disputes about the philosophy of social science (e.g., compare Black, 1972, with Nonet, 1976; Skolnick, 1965, with Auerbach, 1966) or about the "truth" of the consensus/conflict debate (compare Chiricos and Waldo, 1975 with Quinney, 1974, or Chambliss and Mankoff, 1976).

We find these constricted perspectives a disappointment. Failure to be concerned with the structure and content of law and with the rich literature in jurisprudence and legal philosophy leads to a variety of problems. The most elementary (and embarrassing) flows from inattention to the technical detail of law. We recently attended a criminology conference in which two established sociologists of law offered "proof" of the truth of the conflict perspective on criminal law: a quantitative demonstration that a *state* criminal trial court was ignoring the clear requirements of the *federal* (!) speedy trial act. The technical structures and forms of the law, the distinctions and differential hierarchies of power within the law, and the differential contents of legal subjects reflect real differences in what can and will happen. Ignorance of statutory or procedural detail can lead to gravely mistaken conclusions about what is observed in the field. The problem is the basic one .of validity.

Another problem is the breathless criminological rediscovery of long established legal ideas. The entire "crimes without victims" literature tends to demonstrate this problem. Lawyers, for example, find the labelling perspective trivial: the criminal sanction is *supposed* to stigmatize the convict and is *supposed* to alter the convict's situation for the worse. It is only lately (in historical terms) that the criminal law has not made provision for the permanent labelling of at least some offenders through mutilation. And of course, as Michael and Adler (1933) observed almost half a century ago, criminal law is, by definition, the *formal* cause of crime. But, Bentham (1970) made the same point 200 years ago; he also commented on the stupidity of using the criminal sanction to control victimless crimes:

> With what chance of success, for example, would a legislator go about to extirpate drunkenness and fornication by dint of legal punishment? Not all the tortures which ingenuity could invent would compass it: and, before he had made any progress worth regarding, such a mass of evil would be produced by punishment, as would exceed, a thousandfold, the utmost possible mischief of the offence [1970: 320].

There is a further problem which confounds a sociology of North American law. Both the Canadian and American legal systems are (with trivial local exceptions such as Quebec's *code civile* or California's community property law) grounded in and derived from English common law. Yet, the principal North American sociological commentators today usually base their work on the observations of Durkheim, Weber, or Marx, rather than, say, Sumner or Bentley. But Durkheim wrote of *droit* and *loi;* Marx and Weber were concerned with *recht* and *gesetz*—words with very different connotations from the single English word *law.* In addition, the conceptual structures of the Romano-Germanic and Common Law families of legal systems are sufficiently different that lawyers have a great deal of trouble communicating with fellow professionals trained in the other style (David and Brierly, 1968; but compare with Friedmann, 1967: 515-550). Thus, the North American student of legal sociology should use continental European social theory of law with care.

Two points need to be made with respect to jurisprudence. The first is that, with the exception of Quinney's early work (1969: 20-30), insufficient effort has been made to mine or exploit the rich vein of intellectual potential in Pound's sociological jurisprudence (1959) or in the realist jurisprudence which remade American legal education at Chicago, Yale, and Columbia in the 1930s, created modern commercial law, and shaped the theory of trade regulation and consumer protection which forms the basis for contemporary studies in white-collar crime.

The second point about jurisprudence is this: North American legal systems (as well as the English) are dominated by a "ruling theory of law" (Dworkin, 1977), an ideology which guides the possibilities and directions of legal change. The doctrine is the descendant of the Benthamite tradition: as Dworkin would have it, its normative component is the doctrine of utility, its conceptual component is the system of analytic positivism. The works of H.L.A. Hart (1961), and of Packer (1968) are part of this tradition; the American Bill of Rights is part of this tradition. Indeed, the criminal law revolution of the 1960s may even be seen as an unfolding of the ruling theory. Classical criminology is at the core of the ruling theory of law—the current return to certainty in punishment, the moves to judicial control of prisons, proposals for the abolition of status offenses for juveniles—all of these represent a return to what Vold dismissed as "legal and administrative criminology" (1958: 14-26).

The positions taken by scholars working in the tradition of the ruling theory of law have had enormous impact on policy. Neither the empirical arguments of social scientists (Tappen, 1969) nor the arguments of legal moralists like Wigmore (1926) reformed the juvenile court. Arguments drawn from the implications of the ruling theory in terms of utility and fairness brought us *In re Gault* (1967) [Faust and Brantingham, 1979; Kittrie, 1971: 102-168]. Thus, we think that the concerns of scholars working in the tradition of the ruling theory of law must be explored; in particular, the works of Pound and H.L.A. Hart should be considered in an informed sociology of criminal law.

The first two essays in this volume deal with conceptual problems in the construction of a sociology of criminal law. Turk examines six different sociological and jurisprudential conceptualizations of law: the theological; the existentialist; the anarchist; the Marxian; the legalist; and the positivist. In each case he considers the specification of conditions under which law, as a social institution, ought to disappear. He concludes that four of the six conceptualizations are theoretically arid because they assume the perfectibility of human nature or because they assume that social processes cannot be controlled, or both. Such conceptualizations of law deny the necessity or the possibility of a science of social control and cannot, therefore, form the basis for a sociology of law. The remaining conceptualizations of law fail because they picture law as part of a closed system of control. Turk proposes a definition of law as a permanent feature of all societies, an open system of deference and coercion. He develops a number of formal propositions as guides to future research.

Jeffrey argues that much contemporary legal sociology is confused because it has been conceptualized through a linguistically and empirically sloppy use of the word "law" to describe the content of rules in case reports and legislation; *and* to describe the process by which those rules are used by legal actors to decide disputes or modify their own or their clients' behaviors; *and* to describe aggregate behavior patterns of actors within the legal system. He says that this confusion has resulted in a personification and reification of LAW which stultifies research. Jeffrey proposes a new, restrained definition of law as an aide to clearer empirical and theoretical work in the field.

The second group of essays in this book offer empirical studies of major issues in the sociology of criminal law. Lanza-Kaduce, Krohn, Radosevich and Akers explore several issues in the conflict-consensus debate about the social origins of law, the generality of knowledge about legal rules, the character of social support for legal rules, and the social impact of legal rules. They utilize Durkheim's theory of the relationship between social complexity and forms of social solidarity as indexed by law in order to test both the social agreement with and the social impact of three forms of law: constitutional, criminal, and civil. This represents a major advance for legal sociology in that it uses sociological theory to develop a testable model of law which approaches the sophistication of concepts used by legal positivists (i.e., primary and secondary rules) or by legal comparativists (i.e., public administrative law, law of public wrongs, private law). At the same time, this approach translates Durkheim's continental view of law into American terms. They find that both the knowledge of legal rules and the social impact of legal rules vary by the type of law involved. The patterns of these variations are consistent with predictions derived from Durkheim's theoretical stance.

Yeager and Clinard present a study in the development of white-collar crime: the evolution and enforcement of criminal sanctions against water pollution in the United States. They demonstrate an elaborate temporal interplay between public concern about pollution (nonexistent in 1890, intense in 1972), business interest (water was a free resource in 1890, it became an expensive material after 1972), bureaucratic interests and organizational constraints (the Army Corps of Engineers, the Department of the Interior, the Environmental Protection Agency), and intergovernmental jurisdictional issues in the development of legal controls over water polluters. Their study seems to support a pluralist interpretation of law-making and enforcement, but sets the stage for further research to test the issue of social structural biases in the application of criminal sanctions.

The third group of essays explores the question of law-making from a novel viewpoint. Both essays examine proposed legislation that failed to become law. Seitz, a political scientist, looks at federal efforts to develop comprehensive gun control regulations. The Bureau of Alcohol, Tobacco, and Firearms in the Department of the treasury attempted to adopt tough new regulations controlling the record-keeping attendant to the manufacture and sale of firearms. Lobby pressure succeeded in killing the regulations in the relevant committee of the House of Representatives. The committee also cut back on ATF funding. A pro-gun-control congressman then made a motion in the full House which, had it passed, would have reinstated the proposed ATF regulations and restored the cut funding. Seitz explores the dynamics of the House vote on the motion in terms of regional history and culture, lobby pressures on representatives from safe and marginal districts, and in terms of the role of technical expertise. He considers the outcome along a continuum which ranges from open, democratic politics to closed politics conducted by bureaucratic and technical elites. Seitz concludes that the outcome represents a victory for open politics. He interprets the issue in the context of a Weberian model of law.

In contrast, Snider analyzes the failure of an effort to reform the Combines Investigation Act in Canada in the early 1970s. This act is the Canadian equivalent (though weaker) of American antitrust legislation. It is designed to control the more rapacious and piratical forms of big business behavior. Snider traces the development of the act over the course of the twentieth century up to an announcement by the relevant minister of government intention to replace the act with a new, comprehensive Competition Act. She then traces the buildup of business opposition to and the eventual defeat of the proposed replacement act. She interprets the bill's failure in a Marxian conflict perspective.

The last group of essays deals with aspects of the Benthamite, or classical criminology, ruling theory of law. Prevention of crime through general deterrence is a major tenet of the ruling theory. Anderson presents a careful and thorough review of the current state of empirical research into the deterrence questions. She classifies and analyzes the findings of twenty-one major studies and concludes that the general deterrence hypothesis has not yet been empirically verified. Her finding has major implications for the ruling theory of criminal law.

A second major concern of the ruling theory of law is the issue of punishment: its definition, its justification, its use. Ball reviews the major jurisprudential positions on the justification of punishment and proposes a sociologically informed justification grounded in the construction of social reality.

These essays, both individually and taken together, represent a move toward a jurisprudential sociology of law. We find them intellectually exciting and commend them to you.

Austin T. Turk
University of Toronto

1

CONCEPTIONS OF THE DEMISE OF LAW

The scientific, or empirical study of law presupposes that conceptions of law are somehow founded in observable phenomena. Comparative legal, anthropological, and sociological studies further presuppose that the phenomena of law are to be found in a variety of social environments. Whether viewed as distinct types or as points on a continuum of some kind, the "laws"—the legal systems or orders—of different places and times are expected to be comparable. Equivalences and commonalities are sought and found (or imposed) on the assumption that something is always there which can usefully be considered "law." The bedrock assumption has been that research on the phenomena of law is getting at some fundamental regularities, some constants or invariances, in human behavior and relations.

Conceptions of the demise, end, or disappearance of law imply that law is an historically and culturally specific set of phenomena which can become extinct—like a biological species, a social custom, or a particular society. A more complicated variant of this idea is that law can both die and be reborn, disappear and reappear, depending on whether the conditions needed for its existence are met. Like snow appearing under the right conditions of humidity and temperature, law is seen as limited to some range of appropriate social environments which can themselves appear, disappear, and reappear.

Thus, we have the issue: whether legal phenomena are intrinsic to human social life, or else only temporary or

12

occasionally recurring features or adjuncts. Do law and society go together always, for awhile, or sometimes?

ON THE DEMISE OF LAW

There are at least five explicit and perhaps one implicit conceptions of when and why the idea and institutions of law will or may disappear from human social life. The explicit ones include the theological, anarchist, Marxian, legalist, and positivist; the possible sixth derives from existentialism.

Theological

Most major religious belief systems contain either explicit or implicit challenges to the idea of law as a strictly human instrument. Despite efforts by theologians from Augustine (The City of God, 5th century) to Reinhold Niebuhr (1960) to find ways to accomodate religious commitment and political involvement, the genuinely religious person still has a fundamentally tense, even antagonistic relationship with political authorities and legal normative demands. To believe in a divine or suprahuman power and moral authority transcending the power and authority of specific rulers is to retain a measure of independence that can stimulate opposition to them, active or passive. Only to the extent that people are really able to believe in the divinity incarnate of ruling figures, or the more-than-human source or authorization of their rule, can the religious and political aspects of life be reconciled. It follows that as such equations of divine will and secular power break down, with the increasing enlightenment that comes with experienced diversity, skepticism toward clearly human claims and institutions increases. The religious life, either presently or in some future, almost by definition supersedes every limiting political and other material circumstance, including law. Sometime and somehow, it is believed, human life will be free of injustice and evil, and therefore of the causes of political domination, legalisms, and conflict. Law being at best an imperfect means of resolving problems far too great for humans to solve, and at worst a device for deception and manipulation, will end along with all other fallible human creations and illusions.

Existentialist

Although I am unaware of an existentialist formulation of the end-of-law thesis, some themes in existentialist philosophy (see Barrett, 1958; Tiryakian, 1962) do seem to imply the ultimate failure of legal controls because human destiny is unaffected by human interventions. Individuals act in an absurd maze of mindless constraints about which neither they nor others can do anything. One acts, and wills to act, as one must without the possibility of authentic choice. Striving to control, regulate, manipulate, change events is an endlessly repetitive and finally meaningless project in a universe without discernible purpose or pity. Such thinking extended to collective enterprises such as the legal control of social life suggests that the idea of law is itself pointless and that legal institutions are doomed to failure and collapse. All must eventually reduce to nothingness.

Anarchism

To anarchists law is a myth by which political-economic oppression is camouflaged (see Barnet, 1971; Pepinsky, 1978; Sullivan and Tift, 1977). The truth about any formal organization of social life is that a minority is thereby enabled to exploit the majority on a continuing basis. Conceptions of legality merely serve as propaganda to mislead the people into believing that the state exists to serve them, when in fact they are permitted to exist only to serve the state—which means the ruling class. Only truly consensual, egalitarian societies are viable; the only durable social forms are those created directly by the people themselves to meet needs which they know and feel. Any more remote, complicated organization of social life inevitably means bureaucratization, i.e., regimentation, and the concomitant loss of sensitivity of people to one another's needs. The result is alienation, which must eventually reach such a degree that there is no longer enough trust among people for social life to continue. The breakdown of the artificial order of politicized society follows, and the mystifying legalisms are dissipated. When people see the truth, legalisms can no longer exist; the myth has no force when it is not believed.

Marxian

A postulate of Marxian theory is that law is an instrument of (a) relatively peaceful dispute settlement among factions of the ruling class, and (b) oppression of the working classes by the exploiting classes, by mystification of exploitation and authorization of repressive violence (see Chkhikvadze, 1969; Taylor et al., 1973; Quinney, 1974, 1977). Law is specific to precapitalist, capitalist, and—in radically different form—socialist polities. As the capitalist system collapses, the formalism of bourgeois legal institutions is supplanted by the pragmatism of socialist legality. Instead of forcing cases into a formally closed system of pure legal reasoning (by which political-economic realities are excluded from explicit consideration in the judicial process), socialist legality is an instrument by which to raise the political consciousness of the people. No legal principle, rule, or procedure stands when the Party leadership finds that the needs of the socialist transition to communism require overriding legalities in particular circumstances. The replacement of presocialist, bourgeois modes of thinking by socialist awareness and sensitivity is the primary function of socialist law, which thus helps to pave the way to the communist society. As the transition to communism is achieved, the socialist state and, therefore, socialist law are no longer needed and disappear.

Legalist

For those legalists who follow Fuller (1964) in equating law with a "morality of law" that postulates the autonomy and generality of law (applicability of the same rules to diverse cases), and that implies substantive and procedural regard for individual liberties, the decline of autonomy, generality, and individualized justice in the design and functioning of legal institutions is tantamount to the end of law itself. To the extent that predictability and equity are subverted by the pressure for administrative discretion in responding to the competing demands of various interest groups, the idea and reality of law is lost. Features of the welfare state and corporate society are causing "the disintegration of the rule of law in postliberal society" (Ungar, 1976: 192). The welfare state is characterized by "the rapid expansion of the use of open-ended standards and general clauses in legislation, administration, and adjudication" and by "the turn from formalistic to purposive or policy-oriented styles of legal reasoning and from concerns with formal justice to an interest in procedural and substantive justice" (Ungar, 1976: 193-194). Corporate society is characterized by both conservative and revolutionary efforts to avoid the manipulation of social life by imposed rules in the name of the public interest, and to rely instead upon the working customs of those who participate in the internal affairs of particular communities and enterprises. These trends "prepare the way for the return to the custom of each group as the fundamental and almost exclusive instrument of social order" with the concomitant "logic of tribalism" that precludes an idea of right or justice that transcends the demands of the group itself (Ungar, 1976: 238). The return to primitivism may perhaps be avoided by some propitious blending of the "subversion of inequality" needed to persuade people that collective decisions are in truth such, and of the expansion of "an ever more universal consensus about the immanent order of social life" (Ungar, 1976: 240). (Ungar himself clearly prefers progress, but makes a stronger case for the primitivism alternative.) Whatever happens, the law as an autonomous, general, and liberal institution is seen as ending.

Positivist

From Black's (1976) positivist perspective, law is a variable defined as "governmental social control" (itself left undefined), whose absence is anarchy, i.e.,"social life without law, that is without governmental social control" (1976: 123). The amount of law in social life is determined by the joint values of other variables: stratification, mobility, differentiation, culture, organization. Present trends include (1) the decline of private control of resources which, with the increasing mobility of social life, promotes "the increasing equalization of social classes, races, sexes, and ages" (Black, 1976: 133); (2) greater differentiation of functions, resulting in "increasing interdependence across social life" and therefore interchangeability of partners in all kinds of relationships, as people learn to help or gratify one another in diverse situations rather than in person-sepcific relationships that can no longer be sustained across such diversity of circumstances (Black, 1976: 134-135); (3) increasing cultural homogeneity on a world scale, but with diversity across situations: immediacy, not culture-bearing ("always the same person"), is the mode of social interaction (Black, 1976: 135-136); and (4) increasing organization of social life, but decreasing "scope of organization"—the degree to which a group incorporates its members" which means that "privacy is increasing, and subordination has begun to decline (Black, 1976: 136). "With people constantly moving, and constantly making and losing friends and enemies, the life span of disputes shortens, feuding becomes difficult if not impossible, and mediators and tribunals of all kinds lose their importance" (Black, 1976: 137). The outcome is "a situational society" combining features of both "communal" (group-based) and "situational" (individual-based) anarchy. "If these trends continue, then law will decrease. It might even disappear" (Black, 1976: 137).

POSTULATES AND PROBLEMS

The formidable array of thinkers whose ideas have been so briefly sketched differ in many ways, but most importantly (for present purposes) in their postulates regarding (a) the perfectibility of human nature, and (b) the controllability of social processes. If human nature is perfectible, then at some point the science and work of control will be un-needed. If social processes are uncontrollable, then the science and work of control is ultimately impossible. With respect to their perfectability and controllability postulates, the variant end-of-law conceptions differ as follows:

	Social Processes	
Human Nature	controllable	not controllable
perfectible	Marxian anarchist	theological
not perfectible	legalist positivist	existentialist

Within categories there are of course differences in regard to what exactly is meant by human nature and/or by social processes, what is meant by perfectability and/or controllability, and what are the reasons for conclusions about perfectability and/or controllability. For example, while Marxians and anarchists believe that human nature is perfectible and social processes controllable, the Marxians (much as do legalists) assert that control has to be exercised by elites who correctly understand the necessary theory by which control can bring about perfectibility. Anarchists, in contrast, take seriously the notion that the collective, grass-roots wisdom of "the people" can accomplish control spontaneously, allowing human nature to be expressed in its perfection.

For legalists and positivists social processes are, at least in principle, controllable; however, they see control not as the means to perfecting human nature, but instead as the means for enabling imperfect human beings to live tolerably with one another. Differing views on the sources of human imperfectibility lead, of course, to differing strategies for developing and applying a science of control. Legalists tend to favor classic utilitarianism, and to trust the reflective lore of practitioners of the art of control. Positivists are inclined toward determinism, and generally place more confidence in experimental and/or statistical research by detached rather than participant observers.

Clearly, the legalist and positivist positions do avoid denying either the necessity or the possibility of the science and work of control—thus remaining within the bounds of what is presently known about human capacities and propensities. Furthermore, they (as well as the other end-of-law conceptions) are the products of efforts by gifted observers and analysts to understand the factual diversity and change of legal phenomena. Particular legal ideas and institutions have indeed been found to vary, and sometimes disappear or fall into desuetude. Such demonstrated cultural and historical relativity of legal phenomena lends credence to the inference that law itself must or may end. But the inference is unwarranted.

The difficulty is one of conceptualization, not of observation. From the level of detailed analysis of historically and culturally specific legal phenomenon the theorists have jumped to the general theoretical level. Empirical generalizations and projections can logically be addressed only to the phenomenal level at which observations were made. In this case, Ungar and Black have drawn brilliant, though debatable, pictures of major trends in Western civilization—but they have not shown that, or why, the projected end of Western legal systems as depicted must or will probably have the consequences they describe. That Western legal systems are in for politically significant changes appears likely from these analyses. However, neither Ungar's "tribalism" (much less his utopian alternative) nor Black's "situational society" is probable if one (a) defines law so as to maximize, not curtail, its utility as a scientific concept, and (b) casts the analysis in terms of the full range of what is known about human social life, instead of just what is concluded about Western legal and related social trends.

DEFINING LAW

Conceptions of the demise of law are inadequate basically because they begin with excessively literal, unique, and therefore normative definitions of law, formulated at empirically unhelpful levels of abstraction—either too specific or too disembodied. Indeed, both Ungar and Black appear to aim their theoretical fire simultaneously "over and under." Some elements of their respective concepts are too tied to particular legal contexts, while others are too detached from observable dimensions of behavior and social relatedness.

Although Ungar does note the alternatives of seeing law as either "a universal phenomenon" or "a particular kind of modern legal system," he does not succeed in developing a conception of law "that will allow us to distinguish the sense in which law is indeed a universal phenomenon from the ways in which it is distinctive to certain kinds of society" (1976: 49). Instead of an integrated conception, Ungar offers a sorting of the components of law into three *kinds* of law: consensual interaction is assigned to "customary law," coercive hierarchy to "bureaucratic law," and the autonomous morality, or rule of law to the liberal "legal order or legal system" (1976: 49-54). This tripartite idea of law is rendered even less amenable to research use when Ungar (wisely) points out that "the differences among the types of law always remain fluid" (1976: 54).

Black is somewhat more helpful, in emphasizing the variability of law, but does not go on to specify what it is that varies. Unlike Gibbs (1968), for example, Black is a partial positivist who does not try to identify the empirically observable variables comprising law, but stops with the undeveloped notion that law is "governmental social control" (1976: 2). Thus, the researcher has to work out for himself such basic conceptual matters as what is "government" and how "governmental control" differs from and relates to nongovernmental control. Black's definition of law is in principle applicable to any society with a government exercising governmental control (assuming definitional criteria are established). Nonetheless, the indicated evidentiary bases for his generalizations and the tenor of his discussions strongly suggest that his attention is limited to the Western capitalist, liberal democracies—especially the

United States. The projected combination of communes, atomistic individualism, and technologically wondrous degression of spatial and social mobility strikes me as a quintessential American scenario!

Elsewhere (Turk, 1976), I have proposed that the most empirically adequate conception of law is that it is multidimensional power, stressing the idea of *legal control.* Such a conception leads us to look for ways in which the regularized imposition of normative expectations is accomplished by persons whose dominance is grounded in some combination of coercion and deference. Briefly stated, the key propositions are (1) that legal control is intrinsically coercive, no matter how subtly implemented, and (2) that deference is the product of coercion.

Though coercion may be generated in quite subtle ways by psychological and environmental manipulation, in legal control it rests on or lies in "the socially recognized privilege" of threatening/using deadly violence (Hoebel, 1954). In individuals that recognition may issue more from agreement, respect, trust, or expediency, fear, fatalism. Whatever the motivational bases for individual deference, the structural bases for population deference are the mechanisms by which power inequalities are demonstrated and perpetuated. The organization and mobilization of the means of violence underlies and backs up educative and hortatory methods of legal socialization. Over time, people collectively learn "social norms of deference" (Turk, 1969: 43), i.e., to recognize as "privilege" what empirically and logically is no more than assertion on the part of those who *do* threaten and use deadly violence to sustain their claim to be "the authorities" and not just the most powerful decision makers of the collectivity. An extremely important corollary is that the efficacy of "field controls" presupposes the establishment and maintenance of a "field" by sufficient "command controls" (see Feeley, 1976).

Control may, of course, be exercised by persons who are not themselves the wielders of physical force. Legal control may involve varying degrees of specialization. As courts, mediators, police are differentiated (Schwartz and Miller, 1964; Wimberley, 1973), the substantive and procedural normative structures become more complex, as do the problems of ensuring consistency and reducing rivalries in the control process (Boydell and Connidis, 1974). A critical distinction becomes possible: deference may be accorded the persons exercising control or to the positions they hold in the structure of power. The characteristic blending of personal and positional deference may be used to define types of legal systems, somewhat as Ungar (1976) does:

Object of Deference	Type of Legal System
person	situational (e.g., "revolutionary" or "frontier" justice)
person ⩾ position	customary (e.g., "primitive" or "traditional" law)
position > person	liberal democratic (e.g., bourgeois "rule of law" plus "equity")
position	bureaucratic (e.g., "socialist legality" plus "social justice")

However, such gross typologies seem to have only limited value for research because they promote thinking in terms of categorical attributes of *closed* systems instead of variable processes occurring in *open* systems. The first kind of thinking leads to such conclusions as that law ends when one or more of the systems ends; the second kind of thinking leads to propositions about ongoing systemic processes reflecting invariant features of social organization.

INVARIANCES OF SOCIAL ORGANIZATION

The purpose here is not to assert and defend these particular propositions but to indicate formally what appear to be the most promising first statements, as derived from such sources as Collins (1975), Lenski (1966, 1978), LeVine and Campbell (1972), and Rapoport (1974).

(1) Positional differences lead to experience differences, which in turn lead to perceptual and evaluative differences.

There are consequently always problems in any relationship of accomplishing mutually beneficial and nonthreatening contacts (meaning any form of communication or other exchange).

(2) Population growth promotes increasing interaction density, which leads to the decreasing feasibility and effectiveness of interpersonal (intragroup) methods of resolving contact problems.

(3) If secession ("hiving off") is precluded by physical or social barriers, then there will be *clustering* of similarly situated persons (e.g., clans or classes) who develop relatively formal methods of reducing contact problems among themselves, and to promote coordinated actions in dealing with outsiders.

(4) If technological development is sufficient to force specialization of production, then there will be additional pressures to develop more adequate controls for dealing with indirect reciprocal, i.e., functional relationships. The inadequacy of methods appropriate for controlling direct relationships will become increasingly obvious. The new reality, and the more pressing one, becomes that of interdependency without interaction.

(5) Contacts in more indirect relationships are subject to greater variability because of (a) the greater time lag in feedback versus the almost instant feedback in interaction; (b) the greater availability of functional alternatives in a complex system of interdependencies; and, (c) the relatively greater insensitivity/indifference to asymmetrical exchanges and threatening communications when communication is more limited. Contacts tend to be restricted to matters of impersonal exchange excluding concerns about personally "meaningful" relations.

(6) Variability in contacts then leads to greater inequalities, as asymmetrical exchanges are cumulated. *Contra* Ungar and Black, this produces increasing need for *more* formalized, regularized, i.e., *legal* controls to keep the advantaged and disadvantaged from destroying themselves by failing to perform their respective roles in the system of functional interdependencies. Without some division of

function in which recognized persons are able to impose brakes and solutions, the antagonistic relations between groups, or clusters of persons who cannot really "know" and therefore trust kinds of people much different from themselves and their kind would destroy social life.

(7) Contemporary societies are open systems, overlapping and coalescing into something approaching a global society. Given their inclination (as detected by Black) to separate as far as possible, while continuing to exploit one another as much as possible (which are obviously contradictory social processes), the clusters of people comprising contemporary society simply cannot survive without legal controls by which to arbitrate otherwise unresolvable, and inevitable, conflicts among them.

(8) It is highly unlikely that human beings will simply abandon the concept of authority in any "crisis of legitimation" (Habermas, 1975). Rather, new authorities can be expected to replace old ones; any changes will be in power alignments and/or control strategies—not in the rejection of authority itself. The most probable outcome of such crises is a redistribution of resources (power) that is accomplished by, and in turn produces, transformations of legal control structures. Some plausible transformations are:

(a) Any disruption of social structure (by revolution, invasion, technological change, environmental catastrophe, or whatever) reduces or destroys positional deference. Personal deference ("charisma") is however, enhanced by such disruption—if responsibility for the breakdown and attendant troubles can be ideologically or positionally discounted.

(b) The loss of positional deference constitutes a vacuum of authority into which move people having or seeking personal deference.

(c) Persons still possessing the symbols of positional authority attempt initially to claim positional deference. Continued disruption makes it decreasingly likely that such claims will be successful, except for those individuals astute enough to begin discouraging positional deference (asserting "my authority to command your obedience") and seeking personal deference (indicating "my willingness and ability to help solve our common problems").

(d) As increasing contacts create or reestablish social organization, personal deference is weakened as it begins necessarily to be filtered and diluted through chains of contacts.

(e) Internal differentiation of experience, and contacts across group boundaries, soon push people toward greater concentration and centralization of authority—with positional deference becoming an increasingly significant component of authority. With "the routinization of charisma" (Weber, 1968: 246-254, 1121-1123), a new blending of positional with personal deference begins its own unique history of control and challenge.

It should be evident that such propositions point to neither an evolutionary, a cyclical, nor a spiral model of legal order and change. No inevitable progression from one mode of legal control to another is implied, nor any unalterable one-way or periodic rising-and-falling of "systems." Nor is there suggested any ineluctable synthesizing process by which new systems are mysteriously procreated by old systems somehow collapsing on themselves or one another. All that is implied is a conviction that the most empirically fruitful conception of lalw is one that stimulates analyses of how legal authority is created, used, and transformed in specific contexts of power and privilege.

SUMMARY

The issue is whether law and society go together always, for awhile, or sometimes. There are several conceptions (theological, existentialist, anarchist, Marxian, legalist, positivist) of when and why the idea and institutions of law will or may disappear from human social life. All but the legalist and positivist conceptions are untenable for scientific purposes because they postulate (1) the perfectibility of human nature, and/or (2) the uncontrollability of social prcesses.

The legalistic conception as exemplified in Ungar's study and the positivist conception as exemplified in Black's are inadequate because they arrive illogically at general theoretical conclusions after examining limited ranges of data. More specifically, these conceptions fall short because some of their elements are too particularistically defined in terms of Western legal history, while others are too abstractly detached from observable invariant features of human social life.

In contrast, it is proposed that a more empirically adequate conception of law is that of multidimensional power by which legal control is accomplished in the varying blends of personal and positional deference that constitute legal authority. This conception is used in a series of propositions about invariant features of social organization that preclude the termination of legal authority as such, but instead produce transformations of some forms of authority into others.

William Jeffrey, Jr.
University of Cincinnati

2

SOCIOLOGISTS' CONCEPTUALIZATIONS OF LAW:
A Modest Proposal for Paradigm Revision

The modesty of this proposal will be found by readers to be almost unbelievable. Stated in words of one syllable, the proposal is this: Social scientists should stop talking about "the law" in the way they have been talking about it. Instead, they should employ that two-word phrase to refer *only* to those propositions or sentences which are printed as official texts in the statute books or appear in the opinions written by the judges in connection with their decisions of appellate cases. Stated in other words, social scientists should not use the law to refer to what human beings— legislators, judges, counsellors, advocates, prosecutors, and police—do with or to those propositions or sentences or what sundry other humans may say or write about those sentences or propositions. In short, one element of the proposed paradigm is that the law, i.e., those official utterances, be viewed merely as a lifeless gadget, an inert

AUTHOR'S NOTE: *This is a revision of a presentation made at the convention of the American Society of Criminology, Dallas, Texas, 1978. The author is indebted to the panelists and participants at the session, and particularly to Dr. J. Robert Lilly, Associate Professor of Sociology, Northern Kentucky University, for his continued interest and encouragement during the preparation of this essay. The author is also indebted to Dr. Joseph F. Foster, Associate Professor of Anthropology, University of Cincinnati, for kind assistance with relevant literature in the field of linguistics.*

device, or an inanimate tool which simply reposes in those ponderous law books.[1]

A second element of the paradigm is that these lifeless devices and inanimate implements have no influence, impact, or societally significant meaning until some of those persons just mentioned make use of them in particular instances of human behavior, more specifically *but not exclusively* in the sense of "doing something about the trouble situations which arise in the society." The writer emphasizes that the term "situations" is used here as including civil as well as criminal cases. Readers will also have noticed that the state and threadbare idiom which refers to judges' behavior as "applying the law to the facts" is not used here. This greatly overworked phrase not only conjures up distortive images of adhesive band-aids or sticking plaster, but also seriously *over*emphasizes the seemingly monolithic perspective from which "the facts" are seen as being somehow unalterably *given* "out there." This greatly obscures the ambit within which the facts are malleable by counsellors, advocates, prosecutors, and judges.

The first basic reason for proposing this revised paradigm is that its adoption will facilitate a sorting-out of the elements in situations being analyzed. This explicit sorting-out will in turn enable many people—criminologists and sociologists as well as lawyers—to perceive more clearly, and consequently to analyze more accurately and effectively, precisely how the legal system (and the law is only one of the many elements in that system) actually works in its societal context. To whatever extent these results are achieved, the development of sociology of law will be accelerated and enriched—a consequence presumably viewed as desirable by readers of this essay.

There are two additional basic reasons underlying the revised paradigm proposed here. The first reason is this: One result of its general adoption will be that social scientists and, possibly, citizens generally will find it much easier to halt the unproductive confusion of the law with what officials (and others) *do*.[2] In a word, adoption of the proposed paradigm will greatly fortify the recognition that humans, *not* the law, are the only possible actors in society. One potential by-product is that whenever official (or other) behavior is unsatisfactory or inappropriate—and this may be the fact in many situations—then the responsibility for this condition could be clearly and directly imputed to the appropriate human culput, and not deflected or diverted on some innocent lifeless abstraction.

The second reason is this: So long as people (including many social scientists) continue to attribute independent action to some *corpus* of legal rules, then precisely so long will those people and those social scientists too readily assume, believe, or perhaps hope that a change in legal rules will be (promptly) followed by a change in humans' behavior. The massive program of societal experimentation in the sociology of law conducted under federal auspices in this nation for at least the past quarter of a century supplies a host of examples which need no further mention in this essay.

Despite the appealing modesty of the proposal just encountered, the present writer entertains no illusion about its instantaneous approval or prompt adoption. This part of the essay will therefore be devoted to a discussion of a few stereotypes or shibboleths which have somehow grown up around or become entangled with that traditional conceptualization of the law herein nominated to be thrown into an intellectual trashbin. This section is designed to do two things: first, wherever necessary, to assist readers in relinquishing some probably dearly held notions about the law, and second, by juxtaposing the new and the old paradigms, to supply some useful specifics in order to flesh out the bare outlines of the revised paradigm proposed here.

I start from the premise that explanations in criminology or sociology are neither facilitated nor fortified by including or relying on any personification of abstract concepts. The prescription in William of Occam's famous razor against the proliferation of superfluous entities in explanations is particularly relevant at this point. The target of social scientists' efforts to understand is, of course, human behavior, and the present "modest proposal" to deprive the law of all capacity for any self-starting action is offered to assist scientists in maintaining a clear and sharp focus on this fundamental fact. Whenever any situation being analyzed can be purged of *non*human actors, such cleansing will facilitate explanation by reducing the number of actors which must be taken into account. The writer readily agrees that a nonhuman actor will reenter any situation *whenever* the human actors in it give evidence that *they believe* in such a nonhuman participant. In this situation, however, we simply confront one additional piece of human behavior to be explained. The "nonhuman actor" cannot furnish any explanation. People —i.e., living, identifiable humans—must *do* something with those statements and propositions before there is any behavior with which criminologists, sociologists of law, or other scientists should seriously be concerned.

Another barnaclelike intellectual stereotype merits attention here. This particular instance is but one example taken from a trouble-breeding encrustation of attractive but thoroughly deceptive shorthand expressions, whose unscrutinized reiteration by social scientists and lawyers effectively prevents accurate perception of the legal system in its societal context. Most probably, readers have heard or read this proposition: "Law is a command." For this familiar shorthand remark we are chiefly indebted to the long-canonized British legal philosopher, the late John Austin (1954: 13-21). However helpful Austin's view may once have been, the principal vice in it has come to consist in the fact that it regards a correct statement about a relatively very small number of instances as being correct also about the entire mass of those sentences or propositions.

We may consider an example from criminal law. The propositions in this field are not generally cast in the imperative language of command: "Thou shalt not kill."

Instead, the multitude of statutes and judicial opinions constitutes an extremely complicated lexicon, defining the degrees of murder and manslaughter, the elements of burglary or arson, exculpatory elements, defenses, and so on, and so forth. The reader will bear in mind that the target of social scientists' analysis is human behavior—by police, prosecutors, defense counsel, trial judges, jurors, and appellate judges—behavior which is triggered by the butler's discovery of the bloody corpse in the master's elegant library. Any "Austinian" statement or belief that all these people are obeying some "command" is neither clear nor accurate. The present writer will unhesitantly concede that, with some effort, a command might be "constructed" on the basis of the statutory or judicial texts. Nevertheless, the following question will not evaporate: Why should the law be conceptualized in such a way that even this small *quantum* of intellectual gymnastics is necessary? These people are not "obeying a command," they are "coping with a situation."[3] The proffered language suggests that preserving the Austinian idiom of command is not worth its intellectual costs.

This example of murder suggests another point which deserves the reader's attention. Suppose for the moment that we press ahead anyway and "construct" some form of command in this situation. We thereupon confront this unblinkable fact: Our carefully confected command had been obviously and completely ignored—the corpse was still oozing blood when the cops arrived on the scene! Precisely what, the writer asks, has been explained by injecting this command element? Criminal behaviors have several explanations but "violation of a command" is clearly not one of them. In brief, casting these situations in Austinian command idiom does nothing more than make the difference between inert legal rules and active human behavior *seem* larger than it is in actual fact.

The next point may be stated as follows: The law is not *descriptive* of anything.[4] There exists a strong tendency to regard legal propositions ("Offer and acceptance establish a contract") as bearing a close resemblance to scientific propositions in the natural sciences ("Oxygen and hydrogen in certain proportions combine to form water"). This tendency is a cultural residue of the notion, once warmly cherished by many eminent Victorians, that "law is a science." The harmful influence of this tendency is greatly enhanced by its normally unarticulated condition.

Perhaps, some readers are now thinking, "All right, perhaps the law isn't *descriptive.* However, the law is unquestionably *prescriptive* or 'normative.'" That suggestion evokes this response: Whenever people say or believe that the law is "normative," what we are actually being told is that *they regard* law as normative, and so, *for them,* law becomes normative. Not only does the example firmly and clearly connect the law with the social construction of knowledge (Berger and Luckmann, 1966), but it neatly articulates two points which the writer is concerned to emphasize: First, that some quality or some attribute has been *added to* or imputed to those propositions in the law books; and second, that whatever be the quality added by human action, it is *not* an inherent element of any of those propositions and sentences.

With the completion of the foregoing preliminary observations, the writer is in a position to undertake a more affirmative presentation of this modest proposal.

The fact will bear repeating that a very considerable majority of paradigms in the social sciences are most intimately bound up with the very language of their formulation. As a general rule, the natural sciences have a great many more physical or biological referents serving to anchor their conceptual structures than is the case with the social sciences. While such "labels" as "oxygen" or "hydrogen" can be assigned a single univocal meaning, such labels as "property," "contract," or "tort" are used to refer to such a wide spectrum of multifaceted factual situations that any parallel or even roughly comparable univocality is impossible. Obviously, there is no space in this essay for any discussion of the virtually limitless topic of the relations between *life* and *language*.[5] It is essential to the present writer's purpose, however, that at least something be said concerning the immense and fundamental question of the complicated relationships between *language* and *law*.

Every reader is fully aware of humans' need to have a "label" or "designation" for "things" (or "concepts") if the things are to be talked about—indeed, if humans are even to think about them at all. Apart from the workings of the subconscious (a subject the writer gladly relinquishes to the Freudians), whenever a person cannot state his problem in words—if only to himself in the quiet of his own room—that individual does not have, and he cannot get, a "handle" on his problem. Nearly everyone has heard it or said it: "I know what I think; I just can't put it into words." Despite the familiar disclaimer, persons who utter that remark do *not* know what they think. (An exception must be noted to cover the special case of the speaker's fear of uttering obscene or indecent language.)

The writer trusts this example will suggest the indisputably fundamental role of language, not only in law, but throughout the social sciences. Whether or not life is William James' "big buzzing, blooming confusion," situations do not come to an observer, a lawyer, or a social scientist all neatly labelled ready for processing.[6] What a (technical) vocabulary provides are ready-made "linguistic handles" for the facts of situations; indeed, such a vocabulary will in varying degrees "constitute" or "crystallize" or "precipitate" the facts.[7]

At least one other closely related point deserves clear statement: The mere existence of the (technical) vocabulary does not determine *which* particular vocabulary item will be used by a lawyer or a social scientist for the specific situation confronting them for analysis ("diagnosis"). Scientists' choices, of course, many be confined by a vocabulary, but the perception of "congruence" between their "facts" and the vocabulary comes only from the scientists, *not* from the vocabulary.

Linking the immediately foregoing discussion with the law will make explicit several important elements in the paradigm herein proposed. The determination of *which* of all the available labels is appropriate (I do not say "correct") is in large measure what the judicial process is all about.[8] Counsel for the litigants will offer competing selections of labels, chosen with an eye to putting the best possible face on the facts of their clients' cases. Trial judges and juries confront a choice between the proffered labels, as will the appellate judges in their turn.

Thus far, the present writer has urged that the law is neither descriptive nor prescriptive. At this stage, perhaps, some readers will think, "This author must surely agree, however, that 'law regulates human conduct' or that 'legal rules govern human behavior'"—if we may put under scrutiny two more of the traditional paradigms thoroughly familiar to criminologists and sociologists.

The writer will gladly agree, but *only* on condition that in their turn readers will agree to these two points: First, that the Pickwickian use of language is a completely acceptable procedure in science, and, second, that its use does not offend readers' logical or aesthetic sensibilities. The Pickwickian element consists in this stubborn fact: In the great majority of cases, civil as well as criminal, the rules which allegedly "govern" behavior are brought into play *after the fact.* To relate this to the case mentioned earlier, not until that bleeding corpse had been discovered in the library did anybody start using legal rules (i.e., those propositions) to "cope with the trouble situation."

A brief consideration of some instances from civil litigation will advance the inquiry. For our first example, let us consider a commercial contract for shipments of perishable commodities. Suppose—and this may have been more frequently the factual situation in somewhat earlier years— that the parties have not included in their contract any provision about what was to happen (i.e., who should pay how much to whom) in the event that a shipment should be delayed or even fail to arrive at all. Now, some shipment is delayed, and problems are generated. If this "trouble situation" proves (for whatever reason) to be beyond peaceful negotiation by the businessmen concerned, and thereafter blossoms into full-dress litigation, counsel and courts will face the necessity of doing what they can, using whatever official propositions or utterances are then available in the law books, in order to handle ("cope with") the dispute. Any talk about command or "regulating" or "governing", vis-à-vis this type of situation, is clearly irrelevant and obfuscatory.

Consider another familiar area of civil disputes. Does any reader think for a moment that the persons involved in an automobile accident "regulated" or "governed" their behavior with an eye on the rules of tort law? Can anyone believe that it is a useful piece of business for social scientists and jurists to talk about the "victims'" behavior as though these latter had done so?

Again, does any reader suppose that all instances of "intestacy" (where persons have died without a last will and testament) represent deliberate adoptions by the dear departed of the state's statutory provisions for the distribution of their estates? (The relevance of this last example for the command point earlier discussed will not have escaped the reader.) Most probably all readers will agree that no human being is "commanded" to leave behind a last will and testament. Suppose, however—and the case is neither unusual nor infrequent—that some person had died without leaving behind such a document. The resulting "gap" (read: trouble situation) will be coped with by administrators and probate courts using the state's statute on descent and distribution. Viewing these intestacy statutes as embodying any command, when their use can be entirely precluded by any testator who leaves a valid and adequate will, seems to this writer an analytically unproductive exercise.

In short, then, use of the verbs "regulate" or "govern" to designate this *after-the-fact* recourse to rules, vis-à-vis behavior, is neither particularly accurate nor helpful. The reader's attention is also drawn to the obvious point that the two additional formulations are classic examples of reifying "legal rules" or the law into an actor, independent of human participation.

There exists some possibility that readers will interpret the foregoing comments about law regulating or governing human behavior as rather too easily suggesting a greater separation between human behavior and law than is intended. The appropriate qualification, however, can be stated briefly. The law undoubtedly *affects* human behavior, whenever legal rules are explicitly taken into account in planning legal transactions. Instances not flawed by any after-the-fact element will therefore be found in such broad areas as "estate planning," as well as much contract drafting, and deeds, mortgages, and related conveyancing business. And some people do, indeed, find the state's arrangements for intestate succession quite acceptable, and therefore deliberately refrain from making a last will and testament. With its suggestion of a lesser degree of coercion, the verb "affect" thus appears to be more appropriate for those types of situations than such verbs as "regulate" or "govern," with their somewhat "heavier" overtones.

One task remains for the writer in offering this modest proposal for paradigm revision, and that task is to respond to this question probably lurking in readers' minds: What difference would be made by adopting the proposed paradigm? The writer's response is to comment on a brief series of statement by two leading sociologists of law in two of the articles under the rubric of "LAW" in a standard reference work published just over a decade ago (Selznick, 1968; Bohannan, 1968). In no sense are the statements selected for comment offered as a "parade of horribles." Their use here reflects the writer's belief that they are entirely representative products of the paradigm whose revision is proposed herein. To employ the precise language of one of these scholars,

> The major problem of legal sociology remains the integration of jurisprudence and social research. Unless jurisprudential

issues of the nature and functions of law . . . are addressed by modern investigators, the sociology of law can have only a peripheral intellectual importance [Selznick, 1968: 58].

(1) It [i.e., the instrumentalist approach] thus invites close study of what the law is and does in fact. . . . Moreover, law is seen as having more than one function; not only is it a vehicle for maintaining public order and settling disputes, but it also facilitates voluntary transactions and arrangements, [and the like] [Selznick, 1968: 50].

This personification of "law" is misleading shorthand. Law does not do anything; human beings do things. Law is not a vehicle for anything; the "legal system" is the vehicle, which has law (legal rules) as just one piece of its equipment.

(2) The special work of law is to identify claims and obligations that merit official validation or enforcement [Selznick, 1968: 52].

This statement is too highly compressed. Adoption of the proposed paradigm would stimulate a fuller articulation along these lines: Within the legal system, legislators enact statutes respecting claims and obligations, lawyers identify their clients' claims and obligations and assist judges or decision makers (e.g., administrative officials) in validating or enforcing them.

(3) For the most part, legal sociology has viewed law as a passive rather than active agent in social change. Law "responds" to new circumstances and pressures. However, especially in recent years the great social effects of legal change have been too obvious to ignore. The question is no longer whether law is a significant vehicle of social change, but rather *how* it so functions and what special problems arise [Selznick, 1968: 56].

Legal sociology has undoubtedly proceeded as Professor Selznick has said, but was it not correct in viewing law as being those passive statutory and judge-made rules on the law books? In the next sentence, the quotes should be put around law rather than around "responds." Parts of the legal system did whatever responding was done: *Legislators* put new statutes on the books, or repealed old enactments; *lawyers*, whatever the stimuli, saw new possibilities in challenging the "received" meanings of statutes and case-law rules; and *judges* in turn accepted the new rules and the challenges to former rules, or in one way or another qualified their acceptance of these "novelties." In short, the proposed paradigm would make such personification unfashionable, and instead direct researchers' attention to identifiable behavior by specifiable humans—lawmakers, lawyers, and courts. Finally, these changes in legal rules will be "a significant vehicle of social change" only to the extent that citizens (generally, and not only those involved in particular enactments or law suits) believe in, agree with, or accept the changes in the rules *and* thereafter model their behavior in congruence with the new rules. As previously urged, however, this citizens' behavior is something *added to* the printed rules, and is not inherent in them.

Thus, it is the very nature of law and its capacity to "do something about" the primary social institutions that create the lack of phase. . . . It is the fertile dilemma of law that it must always be out of step with society, but that people must always . . . attempt to reduce the lack of phase [Bohannan, 1968: 76].

The difficulty in this passage stems from the reification of law (apparently it has not only a very nature but a capacity as well), which obscures the ineluctable fact that *only* the human beings located somewhere in the legal system have the capacity to do anything about anything. (Whether the legal system is a "primary" or a "secondary" social institution is, like questions of obscenity, in the mind of the participant-observer. *De gustibus non disputandum est.)* As for the "out-of-step" issue, the legal system is, of course, an integral part of the societal order. Whenever some rules are perceived by humans—citizens, legislators, counsellors and advocates, or judges—as being out-of-phase, this is *not* a fact about the rules, but about the humans. The proposed paradigm would simply urge the straightforward recognition of this fact.

The writer's modest proposal for paradigm revision is not offered as being the only paradigm, as some kind of "pure theory of law." The proposal is made for the single purpose of enhancing and facilitating interdisciplinary collaboration between sociologists and lawyers. This general matter of paradigms should be taken a little further. Precisely as sociologists and criminologists recognize competing paradigms in their discipline, so do the jurists, as most readers are aware. While the writer has no idea what the inscrutable future holds in store for the various paradigms in sociology and criminology, he is certain that philosophers of law are no nearer the final resolution of their paradigmatic difficulties than they were when that compulsive questioner, Socrates, held forth on those street corners in ancient Athens. So far as interdisciplinary efforts are concerned, however, this fact is not a matter of great consequence. This is not in any degree to deny the fascination of jurisprudential speculation, but the writer suggests that the way out of the seeming dilemma is to regard the various schools of legal philosophers as engaged in embroidering on a common core, namely, those legal rules contained in statute books or judicial opinions. If the philosophers of law want to get all tangled up in the tantalizing question "What is law?" no serious damage has been done. Meanwhile, criminologists and sociologists will go ahead and concentrate their attention on whatever their fellow humans *do* to or with legal rules, and should the philosophers, perchance, come up with something relevant, social scientists will make use of it where and as may be appropriate.

NOTES

1. The untoward consequences of rejecting this element of the paradigm and, instead, attributing unlimited life, power, and capacity for action to a reified "law"

are conclusively demonstrated in a recent book (Black, 1976). For an extended review of this book, see Jeffrey (1978).

2. Primarily for its shock value fifty years ago, Karl Llewellyn took this position: "What these officials do about disputes is, to my mind, the law itself" (Llewellyn, 1930: 3). Three decades later, however, he elaborated a greatly matured view, in his *magnum opus* (Llewellyn, 1960). This volume is replete with insight based on empirical inquiries on how lawyers and judges make professional or "operational" use of legal rules. The book might with much benefit be included in lists of required reading for graduate students in the social sciences.

3. This use of "coping" is taken from Dession (1955: 22).

4. The authors of a classic textbook in criminology share this view: "But not one of the essentials of burglary refers to something real, in the way the word *cat* refers to something real" (Sutherland and Cressey, 1978: 15).

5. While we often speak of society as though it were a static structure defined by tradition, it is, in the more intimate sense, nothing of the kind, but a highly intricate network of partial or complete understandings between the members of organizational units of every degree of size and complexity. . . .
It is only apparently a static sum of social institutions; actually it is being reanimated or creatively reaffirmed from day to day by particular acts of a communicative nature which obtain among individuals participating in it [Sapir, 1931: 78]. See also Hymes (1961).

6. Language is heuristic . . . in the much more far-reaching sense that its forms predetermine for us certain modes of observation and interpretation.
It is important to realize that language may not only refer to experience or even mold, interpret and discover experience but that it also substitutes for it [Sapir, 1933: 157].

Readers will bear in mind that the "experience" discussed in this essay is of the special kind exemplified in the "experiencing of abstract concepts," when there are no *physical* referents available. There is an important change in the level of abstraction, when one goes from "Cornelius Tucker" to "independent contractor." No one has ever *seen* an "independent contractor."

7. On this matter of "definitions," there is a relevant discussion in Burling (1970: 78-81). The fascinating problems involved in conceptualizing the process of getting from "sensory data" (e.g., the client in the lawyer's office and what his narrative conveys) to a "perception" of the legal conceptual categories involved ("What you have, Sir, is a problem in 'anticipatory breach of contract'") are perceptively discussed in a article by Kuhn (1961).

8. Many years ago an economist-turned-law-professor published a superb essay on this subject. One particularly relevant passage will bear quotation at this point:

The web of the law is woven with words, yet verbal symbols never carry meaning with precision. . . . Verbal currency passes most uncertainly from country to country and between the generations. As a result precedents may be made to compel where they were never intended to apply; but "ignorance is a great law reformer", and judges often assume that their predecessors were men of sense and reason such as themselves and endow with current meaning the rules by which they are bound. . . . Nor are "the rules of law," with which jurists ply their trade, automata which strip from judgment its choice [Hamilton, 1932: 452].

Lonn Lanza-Kaduce
Marvin D. Krohn
Marcia Radosevich
Ronald L. Akers
University of Iowa

3

LAW AND DURKHEIMIAN ORDER
An Empirical Examination of the Convergence
of Legal and Social Definitions of Law

One of the main theoretical problems in the study of deviance and law-breaking focuses on how and why behaviors come to be socially defined as legal or illegal (Akers, 1968). Two major competing perspectives have developed to explain the nature of the definitional content of law. The dominant sociological view today is some form of the conflict model which posits that there is a conflict of values and actions in society with the more powerful group (or groups) most likely to see its definitions embodied in the law (Chambliss, 1974). In opposition is the consensus model which argues that public policy and legal enactments reflect a societywide normative consensus.

Despite their attempts to account for law's definitions socially, scholars of both the consensus and conflict camps frequently ignore the underlying realities of the formal legal definitions such as the difference between criminal and

AUTHORS' NOTE: *The research was conducted while the authors were on the research staff of The Boys Town Center for the Study of Youth Development (Boys Town, Nebraska). We gratefully acknowledge the support of the center and express our appreciation for the fine cooperation extended to us by its staff.*

civil law. There is, however, a consensus theorist who attaches significance to the bifurcation of law in terms of the nature of the normative order the respective branches of law reflect. Our intention is to investigate the attitudinal concomitants of the various areas of law in light of the theoretical guidance provided by Emile Durkheim.

DURKHEIM'S "THEORY" OF LAW

Unlike most theorists, Durkheim distinguishes between types of law so that the resulting comparative definitions of criminal and civil law violations coincide with legal realities while having extralegal referents. While the type of law was not one of the major theoretical concepts in the *Division of Labor*, it did appear as an indispensable variable in Durkheim's investigation of the relationship between societal complexity (simple versus differentiated) and social solidarity (mechanical versus organic). Indeed, criminal and civil law (with their attendant sanctions) were used as the indices of the types of solidarity (Durkheim, 1933: 64). It was because Durkheim saw solidarity itself as an emergent moral phenomenon, primarily located in society, that he focused on a societal variable like law rather than on individual sentiments. However, to justify his use of criminal and civil law as the proxy variables for mechanical and organic solidarity, it was necessary for Durkheim to offer some detail outlining the association he saw between type of law and the cohering moral order. To do this, he was forced to recognize that the types of solidarity had corresponding levels of feeling states in individuals (Durkheim, 1933: 56, 67, 79-80, 105-106, 226-229). Moreover, because the domain of ethics was seen to be an integral part of the domain of law (Durkheim, 1933: 426-427), it is not surprising that he defined criminal versus civil law largely in terms of evaluative attitudinal referents. It is because of this that the association between normative attitudes and legal definitions has theoretical significance.

Criminal Law

The nature of the consensus posited by Durkheim varied depending on the type of societal cohesion. Durkheim was most explicit in the case of mechanical solidarity. Because mechanical solidarity was borne of the similarity and likeness of the commonly held collective conscience, it had certain features which were definitionally related to its proxy variable, the criminal law. Criminal definitions were "graven in all consciences, everybody knows them and feels that they are well-founded" (Durkheim, 1933: 74). Accordingly, we would hypothesize a high degree of knowledge about criminal law definitions across society and we would expect a high degree of legitimacy to be attributed to them. Moreover, Durkheim (1933: 80) states "that an act is criminal when it offends strong and defined states of the collective conscience." Derivatively, criminal violations should not only be considered morally wrong by the large majority of the population, but they should be considered to be very wrong. Durkheim argues that there is consensus about the intensity of moral feeling that accompanies criminal definitions. (See also Chambliss, 1974). However, because crime does exist and is normal in society, Durkheim proposes a consensus that is something less than unanimous (Durkheim, 1933: 103; see also Simpson, 1963: 61-64). In addition, because the collective conscience has been offended and is in need of explanation, the appropriate sanction is repressive punishment rather than restitution (Durkheim, 1933: 69, 85-103). So, although "the penal reaction is not (always) uniform" in cases of criminal law violations (Durkheim, 1933: 101), we would expect repressive sanctions to be advocated.

Finally, it is this expiatory or retributive nature of sanctioning on behalf of the collective conscience that raises the issue of the "declaratory argument"; that is, does the law's declaration of a norm lend symbolic support to that norm and tend to induce agreement with it and conversely does the removal of the law undermine support for the norm (Walker, 1964; Walker and Argyle, 1964).[1] Because

Durkheim posited widespread consensus in criminal law matters antecedent to the formal legal enactment, criminalizing an existing norm has less significance for his analysis than does decriminalizing a behavioral standard. Durkheim showed greater appreciation than did Sumner (1906) for the complexity of the relationship between law and custom and recognized that law would act back on and affect folkways (see Durkheim, 1933: 83, 84, 476).

Derivative from a Durkheimian analysis and central to the declaratory argument is the issue of what happens when law's symbolic power is removed—when a criminal law is repealed. Bankston and Cramer (1974: 258) state that the "Durkheimian perspective would lead us to suspect that, if the reaction of society becomes less severe, the consequence would be a lessening of social solidarity and commitment to the norm" (see also Gusfield, 1968: 55). A withdrawal of the authoritative symbol of unity by decriminalization would be a serious assault on the mutuality of common beliefs. It is a reasonable extension to hypothesize, therefore, that a change in normative attitudes might accompany repeal of the criminal proscription. More specifically, conduct that was once morally condemned might be less severely evaluated, less severe sanctions might be advocated, and legitimacy might be withdrawn after people learn that the criminal proscription has been removed or that the behavior is not legally proscribed. On the other hand, when a widespread consensus is reaffirmed by announcing criminal proscriptions already anticipated, little attitude change would be expected.

Civil Law

Durkheim was less clear, and perhaps contradictory, about the definitional relationship between civil law and features of organic solidarity. In order to achieve organic solidarity, Durkheim saw the need for an underlying consensus among parts (1933: 360); our specialized relations resulting from the division of labor had to be regulated

(1933: 353-373). However, unlike criminal law proscriptions, civil law definitions did not need to correspond to any sentiment in a majority of us (1933: 112). Nevertheless, they did have some generality due to the functions they fulfilled and it was from opinion that their authority was derived (1933: 127). Indeed, the rules of conduct embodied in the civil law were thought to have grown from the habits and customs of the mutual dependence from which organic solidarity arose (1933: 366). However, the relationship between law and custom was not a simple one; "very often the law cannot be detached from the customs which are its substratum, nor the customs from the law which realized and determines them" (Durkheim, 1933: 426). For example, contract law—the juridical expression par excellence of the cooperation underlying organic solidarity (1933: 123)—determines in a very real way consequences of relations not contracted for and imposes duties and obligations in addition to those negotiated (1933: 214). It is the willingness of society to intervene to order diverse relations such as in contracts that allows Durkheim to consider organic solidarity as a societal phenomenon; society has a stake over and above the interested parties in a dispute because it feels the repercussions (1933: 155). Civil law is the organization of social life (1933: 65) that benefits society's members and accordingly wins their support except where it forces a division of labor that does not reflect their natural differences (1933: 373-388). The nature of the consensus in organic solidarity is based more on the recognized functional interdependence among people than on specific value agreement. This renders the task of hypothesizing more difficult.

While, on one hand, civil law definitions are not seen to reside in commonly held sentiments, on the other hand some generality is expected due both to functions civil laws perform and to the customs from which they derive. Consequently, the degree of knowledge about civil law is less predictable than it was in the case of criminal law. It can be hypothesized with confidence that there should be less knowledge about civil law definitions than there is about criminal law ones. Whether the majority is knowledgeable about a particular civil law probably depends more on the specific subject of the law itself (Durkheim, 1933: 127), that is, how it fits in the nexus of functional interdependency. Nor can one expect legitimacy to be attributed to the legal norm unless its legal status is known. Accordingly, legitimacy might be expected to be lower when the legal status of a norm is unknown. However, when the legal status is supplied, the legitimacy attributed to it should be high because the civil law is the means by which the diverse interdependent relations of society are ordered to the benefit of all. Moreover, because civil law breaches do not correspond to very active sentiments (1933: 127), the level of moral condemnation would be expected to be less severe and less consensual than it was for criminal law violations. In addition, because civil breaches impair the functioning of well-ordered relations, the purpose of any sanctions are primarily to restore smooth operation of the system; they are restitutive, therefore, and not expiatory (1933: 111).

What effect the declaratory argument would have on attitudes circumscribed by civil law is open to alternative interpretations. It may be argued, consistent with Durkheim, that because civil law addresses issues of less moral importance than does criminal law, governmental action, being symbolic of public authority, would be more influential in altering normative attitudes about these less central matters. Alternatively, because civil law enjoys far less evaluative consensus to begin with and is instrumental in integrating via restitution rather than through the expression of public outrage, altering a civil law prescription may have less impact on relevant attitudes than would criminalization or decriminalization. Actually, both approaches may be accurate depending on the particular attitude under consideration. Zeitlin (1968: 268-269) argues that Durkheim restricted morality to those norms which occasion repressive, penal-like sanctions. Accordingly, *moral* condemnation is most closely linked to criminal-like norms in a

Durkheimian analysis so that people's moral evaluations might be relatively indifferent to and unaffected by official civil law definitions. However, because civil law definitions and sanctions help to order and restore diverse or disrupted relations, the government as a recognized integrating mechanism may exert more influence in civil law matters on "nonmoral" normative attitudes like legitimacy or sanctioning preferences. Therefore, we expect shifts in legitimacy and advocated sanctions consistent with the civil law when people are informed of its normative stance on the matter in question, but we anticipate stability in the moral evaluations of civil law matters.

Constitutional Law

Even though Durkheim subsumed constitutional law under the civil law rubric, we have isolated it for separate consideration because its role in the American legal system does not correspond to the continental tradition with which Durkheim was familiar. To Durkheim constitutional law determined both what normal governmental functions are and what their relations among each and with other functions in society should be (1933: 126). Accordingly, it was logically considered to be part of the civil law which reflected organic solidarity because it ordered diverse relations. While this encompasses one of the primary thrusts of constitutional law, such a conceptualization fails to entail the body of law proscribing limitations on government encroachment of individual liberties such as are enumerated in the Bill of Rights. It is this second major theme of American constitutionalism that warrants separate examination. To the extent that the Bill of Rights (and certain of the other amendments) represents our dedication to the individual and his/her civil liberties, such constitutional provisions may assume a unique role in a Durkheimian analysis.

(As organic solidarity progresses in advanced societies) common conscience is (not) threatened with total disappearance. . . . There is even a place where it is strengthened and made precise: that is the way in which it regards the individual . . . the individual becomes the object of a sort of religion. We erect a cult in behalf of personal dignity [Durkheim, 1933: 172].

It seems that the emphasis of constitutional provisions on individual liberties would be viewed by Durkheim as a modern facet of the collective conscience which was associated historically with mechanical solidarity. Accordingly, this theme of constitutional law may be more akin to criminal law than to civil law and should enjoy a high degree of consensus. People would be expected to have as much knowledge about constitutional matters as criminal ones; they should be more informed of protected civil liberties than they are of civil law relations. We might expect the moral condemnation extended to unconstitutional actions to be more like that of criminal violations than the less severe evaluations accorded to civil law breaches. In addition, given the posited consensus, a high degree of legitimacy should be attributed to constitutional law provisions protecting human rights. However, the expected relationship between civil libertarian safeguards and sanctions is more problematic. While the emphasis on the individual may be an expression of the modern collective conscience, it does not contribute to mechanical solidarity like criminal law does. If repressive sanctions express a mechanical solidarity associated with the law of property and inheri- group (1933: 106), they would be inappropriate for a body of law which emphasizes individualism. Indeed, individualism and the commonality of mechanical solidarity are opposing forces (1933: 129-130). Inasmuch as constitutional law that safeguards individual rights dictates what government must refrain from doing, it produces negative or abstentive relations resembling those of the negative solidarity associated with the law or property and inheritance and the law of delicts and quasi-delicts (torts) (see 1933: 115-119). Because restitutive sanctions are associated with negative solidarity for these other law areas, the same might be expected in the instance of constitutional law.

There is room for extending Durkheim alternatively on the relationship of the declaratory statement to civil rights constitutionalism. On the one hand, it is reasonable to think that beliefs residing in the collective conscience would relate to the sense of justice of those societal members who subscribe to them (see Lukes, 1972). Indeed, regulation to the contrary was seen as "forced" and could give rise to conflict. Accordingly, it would be consistent with Durkheim to expect that governmental interference with libertarian norms would be resisted. Following this line of reasoning the moral evaluations of, the sanctions advocated for, and the legitimacy attributed to norms embodied in constitutional safeguards would not change due to government withdrawal of these protections. However, there are countervailing considerations. To the extent that government comes to symbolize public authority, its actions may exert influence over individual sentiments. According to this emphasis, shifts might be expected in normative attitudes due to learning of government postures taken on various libertarian norms. While no a priori predictions can be made with confidence, the data may shed some light on the relationship between government action and attitudes.

Summary of Hypotheses

Five sets of contrasting hypotheses addressing the issues of legal knowledge, legitimacy of the norm, moral evaluation, advocated sanction, and changed evaluations when the official legal definition is removed or provided, can be derived from Durkheim. First, we would expect a high level of knowledge about criminal law and constitutional law and a lower degree of knowledge about civil law norms. Second, the legitimacy attributed to criminal and constitutional law definitions should be high; that accorded to civil law definitions should be low when the legal status of the norm is unknown but it should increase markedly and approach the legitimacy accorded criminal and constitutional definitions when the legal status of the civil law rule is provided. Third, criminal and constitutional law violations should be severely condemned morally by a broad range of people; civil law breaches should reflect less consensus. Fourth, the sanction advocated in the case of violations of criminal law definitions should be more repressive while those favored for civil and constitutional law breaches should be more restitutive.

The fifth set of hypotheses investigates the effects on normative attitudes of being informed that a legal norm either does or does nor apply to a situation. For criminal matters, when the criminality of behavior is confirmed, normative attitudes will remain unchanged; however, when it is stated that the behavior is not criminal, moral evaluations and sanctioning preferences should be moderated and legitimacy withdrawn. For civil law concerns, only non-moral attitudes (legitimacy and advocated sanctions) will be altered consistent with the position adopted by the law (i.e., law or no law). No certain hypotheses could be offered for civil libertarian constitutional situations.

METHODOLOGY

Sample

Data were collected on an adolescent sample drawn from a population of seventh through twelfth grade boys and girls enrolled in two junior high schools and one senior high school in a midsized Iowa community (approximately 60,000) and from a college sample from a midwestern university. The 414 adolescent respondents represent 77% of those in the selected classes. The college sample was composed of 240 students enrolled in four introductory sociology courses that satisfied general social science requirements at the university. Participation for both samples was voluntary and only those present on the day of administration completed questionnaires. Later, two more college classes were used to form a control group (N = 120I) in order to examine testing effects.

Measurement of Variables

Part I of the questionnaire presented six vignettes describing conduct that had legal relevance although not all of the activities were unlawful. The vignettes included two examples from criminal, civil, and constitutional law areas. The criminal law vignettes described an arson situation revolving around the transferred intent of a person whose careless, indifferent conduct with regard to some gasoline resulted in catching a building afire and a conspiracy story where two persons made extensive plans to steal but did not act on them. The civil law matters included a landlord-tenant problem where the renter moves out without providing notice and a labor example where the employer dismisses and does not rehire striking workers. Both of the civil law relationships are specifically mentioned by Durkheim as being germane to organic solidarity (1933: 124-125). The constitutional law area focused on the procedural due process violations committed by a public school principal in expelling a student and on the search and seizure tactics of a police officer in a traffic encounter.

Each vignette was followed by questions on the morality (five-point scale ranging from very right to very wrong), legal legitimation of the rule (whether or not the law should exist), legality (whether the law does exist), and the advocated sanction (ordinal response categories which were later collapsed into repressive and restitutive categories). Part I of the questionnaires was collected on its completion and prior to respondents answering Part II.

The same vignettes were repeated in Part II. The control group was asked to morally evaluate the behaviors, assess the rules' legitimacy, and indicate the appropriate sanctions once again with no additional information provided. The moral evaluation, legitimacy, and advocated sanction questions were repeated for the experimental group as well. However, on half of the vignettes (the arson, rent, and due process situations) the respondents were first told that the behaviors in question violated the criminal, civil, or constitutional law and for the other three situations (the conspiracy, labor, and search vignettes) the respondents were told that the conduct did not violate the relevant area of law. This permitted us to investigate law as an independent variable particularly when responses were controlled for by the knowledge perceptions obtained in Part I. By providing information that a behavior was either lawful or unlawful, we could manipulate people's perceptions of the legal status of the norms and simulate either decriminalization or criminalization to study the respective effects on normative attitudes.

In presenting this manipulation, two questions arose: (1) Would such a short time span between the initial presentation and this manipulation of legal knowledge preclude any chance of a significant treatment effect? (2) If change did occur, could we attribute it to a treatment effect or to a systematic testing effect? We are able to address these issues with preliminary analysis of the data.

First, we did indeed observe a significant change in the expected direction in legitimation, advocated sanction and moral evaluation for some of our vignettes after explicitly stating whether or not the behavior was against the law in our high school and college sample. Second, to investigate whether these changes were indeed due to the manipulation (treatment) or simply an artifact of the testing procedure, we utilized the control sample of college students. With this comparison sample the questionnaires were administered the second time without any information given regarding the legal status of the behavior; rather the vignettes were simply repeated in their original form. Overall, we did not observe much variation between the responses to the first and second presentation among the control group. Only one of eighteen possible before and after measures taken among the control respondents was significant at the .001 level; ten or eighteen comparisons were significant for the treatment group.[2] When mean change scores for the control group are compared with mean change scores for the treatment group (the high school and first college sample) on the eighteen items, we found that for eight of the comparisons the treatment effect is significantly greater than any change in the control group. Four more treatment-control differences reach significance if a more lenient decision-rule about the critical value ($\alpha = .10$) is accepted. In those instances where there is not a significant difference, it is generally due to the fact that the manipulation did not have a significant effect rather than there being very much change on the mean change scores for the control group.

Results and Discussion

Tables 1 through 4 present data relevant to the five sets of hypotheses advanced earlier. Our first hypothesis predicted that our sample would have more accurate knowledge of criminal and constitutional law items than it would have of civil items. With one exception our hypothesis is confirmed by the results presented in Table 1. The extent of legal knowledge concerning the conspiracy item is lower than we anticipated. However, in spite of this the mean percentage of those with accurate knowledge of criminal and constitutional law items is still significantly greater than that for the civil law items.

In examining our second hypothesis concerning the legitimacy extended to the legal norm (whether or not the norm should be embodied in the law), we again observe the same pattern (Table 1). That is, while the mean percentages for the combined criminal and constitutional law items are significantly greater than for the civil law items, the conspiracy item elicits less consensus on the legitimacy of the legal norm. Overall, however, the Durkheimian hypotheses about legitimacy were supported.

Because support for the hypotheses derived from Durkheim's theory of law presented in the *Division of Labor* would be stronger except for the conspiracy item, it warrants further investigation. Conspiracy may be an aberrant criminal law item despite its general moral condemnation (see Table 2) because one of the elements of criminal definitions to Durkheim was precision. (see Durkheim, 1933: 79). Because of uncertainty as to when conspiracy consti-

TABLE 1
Extent of Legal Knowledge and Legitimacy of the Norm
Before Being Informed of its Legal Status
(in percentage)

Type of Law	Knowledge Perceptions			Legitimacy	
	Correct	Didn't Know	Incorrect	Legitimate	Illegitimate
Criminal Law:					
Arson	70.2	12.0	17.8	77.0	23.0
Conspiracy	42.5	11.5	46.0	39.6	60.4
average	56.4 [a]	11.8	31.9	58.3 [b]	41.7
Civil Law:					
Rent	33.6	13.7	53.8	33.3	66.7
Labor	45.6	19.8	34.6	49.0	51.0
average	39.1	16.7	44.2	41.1	58.9
Constitutional Law:					
Due Process	66.7	8.5	24.8	75.8	24.2
Search	66.0	8.4	25.6	76.7	23.3
average	66.4 [c]	8.4	25.2	76.2 [d]	23.8

a. Significantly greater than the average for civil law items (P $<$ .001; T = 12.63; df = 653).
b. Significantly greater than the average for civil law items (P $<$ .001; T = 5.43; df = 653).
c. Significantly greater than the averages for both criminal law (P $<$ .001; T = 6.69; df = 653) and civil law (P .001; T = 17.86; df = 653).
d. Significantly greater than the averages for both criminal law (P $<$ .001; T = 11.16; df = 653) and civil law (P $<$ .001; T = 16.61; df = 653).

tutes a completed criminal act, conspiracy is considered by legal students to be inchoate and accordingly it is this feature that may have rendered responses somewhat aberrant.

In Table 2 it can be seen that constitutional and criminal law violations were considered to be very wrong morally about twice as often as was the case for civil law breaches (64% and 52% to 27%). Over three-fourths of the respond-

TABLE 2
Moral Evaluations of the Described Conduct Before Being
Informed of the Legal Status of the Norm Involved
(in percentage)

Type of Law	Very Wrong	Somewhat Wrong	Neither Right Nor Wrong	Somewhat or Very Right
Criminal Law:				
Arson	55.9	34.6	8.8	0.8
Conspiracy	48.5	28.6	18.7	4.2
average	52.2[a]	31.6	13.7	2.4
Civil Law:				
Rent	29.0	49.8	14.7	6.4
Labor	24.7	26.1	15.1	34.1
average	26.9	38.0	14.9	20.3
Constitutional Law:				
Due Process	79.9	17.5	0.8	1.8
Search	47.9	29.2	9.9	13.0
average	63.9[b]	23.4	5.4	7.4

a. Significantly greater than the average for civil law items (P $<$ .001; T=16.60; df=653).
b. Significantly greater than the average for civil law items (P $<$ .001; T=19.37; df=653).

ents thought each of the criminal and constitutional law violations were wrong or very wrong (indicative of wide normative consensus) while less than two-thirds thought the civil law breaches were wrong. Unlike the knowledge and legitimacy questions, moral evaluations to the conspiracy vignette were not so markedly different from those of the other criminal law item. When significance tests were performed on the differences in means for the respective areas of law, only the difference in moral evaluations between constitutional and criminal law areas failed to reach significance at the .001 level. Again, these findings are exactly what the hypotheses led us to expect: the moral condemnation in both criminal and constitutional matters is strong and more severe than in civil law relations.

TABLE 3

Sanctioning Preferences by Nature of the
Sanction Advocated in Response to Described Conduct
(in percentage)

Type of Law	Nothing	Restitutive Sanctions	Repressive (Penal) Sanctions
Criminal Law:			
Arson	7.1	56.5	36.4
Conspiracy	82.0	--	18.0
average	44.6	--	27.2
Civil Law:			
Rent	58.1	38.1	3.8
Labor	43.9	48.1	8.1
average	51.0	43.1	5.9
Constitutional Law:			
Due Process	4.9	91.1	4.0
Search	12.5	81.0	6.5
average	8.7	86.0	5.2

While Table 3 does not provide evidence of a widespread advocacy of repressive sanctions for criminal law violations, it does indicate that repressive sanctions are much less likely to be advocated for civil and constitutional breaches than for criminal violations. On reexamination of Durkheim, this relative preference for repressive sanctions in criminal matters is all that should have been expected. To Durkheim, the function of the repressive sanction was to restore and reinforce mechanical solidarity. In a modern industrial society like our own, cohesion would flow from the division of labor rather than from the collective conscience; repressive sanctions lose much of their primacy or organic solidarity replaces mechanical solidarity. As a result of this and the continued rationalization of punishment that Durkheim predicted would accompany the rise in organic solidarity, repressive sanctions may be advocated less frequently than formerly. (See Durkheim, 1933: 287-291 and Durkheim, 1973).

Although tangential to a Durkheim analysis, another aspect of the advocacy of sanctions worth noting was the wide agreement among the respondents about the appropriateness of "specific performance" remedies rather than money damages for constitutional violations. Specifically, the oft-attacked "exclusionary rule" (unconstitutionally seized evidence cannot be introduced at trial) was the sanction of choice for the unconstitutional search by the wide majority of young people (60% of the sample) indicating, perhaps, that its merits are more appealing when juxtaposed against alternative remedies than when discussed in the abstract. Specific performance in the way of expunging the school record was nearly unanimously advocated (90% of the sample) in the due process example.

In addition to examining the frequency data to assess the extent of consensus on given normative attitudes for a particular law area, we also calculated the degree of dispersion of the responses in order to obtain another indicator of consensus. Variances will be small and indicate less dispersion or more consensus about responses unless they are unduly inflated by extreme scores. After combining responses for both vignettes for each of the three law areas into single civil, criminal, and constitutional law measures, significance tests for the differences between variances of correlated samples were computed (see Taylor, 1972). In line with our predictions, the degree of consensus in moral evaluations as measured by the variances for criminal (T = 3.724, df = 652) and constitutional law matters (T = 4.561, df = 652) is significantly greater than that for civil law items (P<.001). Also, as was expected, the variance of the constitutional law area did not vary significantly from that for criminal law (T = .802, df = 652). However,using this method of assessing the degree of consensus on the legitimacy measures did not yield significant differences among any of the law areas. Nonstandardized response alternatives for the sanctioning question across

TABLE 4

Changes Occurring in Moral Condemnation, Legitimacy,
and Advocated Sanction After Being Informed
of the Legal Status of the Norm
(in percentage)

Type of Law (Information Provided- Law or no Law)	Morally Very Wrong	Norm is Legitimate	No Sanction	Restit- utive Sanction	Repressive Sanction
Criminal Law:					
(Law) Arson	- 5.3	+12.2[a]	-3.1	+0.6	+2.4
(No Law) Conspiracy	-25.6[a]	-15.6[a]	+5.4[b]	--	-5.5
Civil Law:					
(Law) Rent	- 1.1	+38.6[a]	-25.0	+20.8[a]	+4.3
(No Law) Labor	- 1.7	- 0.8	+ 6.8[a]	- 5.0	-1.9
Constitutional Law:					
(Law) Due Process	- 1.2	+14.3[a]	- 1.0	- 4.4	+5.4
(No Law) Search	- 7.4	- 2.5[a]	+ 8.5[a]	- 7.4	-1.1

a. Change scores showed a significant difference from the pretest at the P < .001 level.

b. The change was significant at the P < .01 level.

the six law items prevented using this approach to assess the consensus on sanction preferences by area of law.

Our final set of hypotheses investigated the declaratory argument. The propositions concerned what effect providing information that a legal norm either did or did not exist to proscribe the conduct in question would have on evaluations of legitimacy of the law, moral evaluation of the conduct, and advocated sanctions. As predicted the only major shift in moral evaluations (significant at the .001 level, T=-11.26, df=557) occurred when respondents were informed that there was no law proscribing criminal conduct (Table 4). Over one-fourth of the sample moved from viewing conspiratorial behavior as very wrong to a more tolerant moral assessment after being told that the conduct did not constitute a crime.[3] Only slight changes occurred when respondents were informed that norms applicable to the labor and search situations were not incorporated into civil and constitutional law. As suspected, informing the respondents that legal norms did exist in the arson and rent examples had almost no effect on the subsequent moral evaluations; nor did knowledge alter moral assessments for the due process situation.

When nonmoral normative attitudes were discussed previously (legitimacy and advocated sanctions), our hypotheses were more uncertain. However, recall that Durkheim posited a widespread consensus prior to the formation of criminal law definitions and that we deduced that there would be similar prior agreement for civil libertarian safeguards. This consensus led us to expect no substantial shift in nonmoral normative attitudes when people were informed of the existence of criminal norms although we were more cautious in predicting about constitutional standards. The results presented in Table 4 support our interpretation for the advocated sanction measures. There was no significant change in sanctioning preferences for the arson example even though the shift to repressive sanctions for the due process item was significant ($P<.001$; $T = 5.38$; $df = 562$). The increase in the percentages of those extending legitimacy was greater than anticipated and statistically significant for both the arson ($P<.001$; $T = 5.79$; $df = 574$) and due process ($P<.001$; $T = 6.52$; $df = 572$) situations. However, the shifts for the civil law rent item were even greater. After learning of the civil law norm 40% of the respondents who thought that no legal standard should exist changed their minds.[4] The shift in sanctioning preferences for the civil law rent item was nearly as dramatic. Of the sample 25% ceased to believe that nothing should happen to the renter and advocated some sanction (usually restitutive) on learning that a civil law norm existed. Our hypothesis that due to the lack of consensus in civil law matters the authority embodied in the law should produce marked changes in nonmoral attitudes toward consistency with the civil law position when people are informed of the law's existence was clearly supported by our data.

In the opposite context (that is when the respondents were told that a legal standard did *not* exist to proscribe the conduct described in the vignettes) there were limited but significant changes in the sanctions advocated for all three law areas. The shifts in legitimacy for the labor and search were small but that for the search was statistically significant ($P < .001$; $T = 3.80$; df = 558). However, more than 15% of the sample moved from attributing legitimacy to withholding it for the criminal law item after being told that the conspiratorial behavior was not illegal ($P < .001$; $T = 8.45$; df = 555).

From the foregoing, it must be concluded that law qua law operates as an independent variable. Learning of the legal status of a norm affected related normative attitudes in a way that was not uniform across all law areas but varied by whether the norm addressed a criminal, civil, or civil libertarian constitutional law matter. The removal of a criminal law proscription potentially relaxes moral views about the formerly prohibited behavior. This has not been demonstrated for civil and constitutional law provisions. Withdrawing the legal standard was also shown to affect the legitimacy extended to the norms and what sanctions were advocated in the event of breach for all of the law areas. When the opposite context was examined—informing respondents of the existence of legal norms regulating specified conduct—the greatest effect occurred in the civil law area. While moral evaluations remained largely unchanged for all law areas in this context, the most striking shifts in legitimacy and advocated sanction occurred with the civil law item. Notable, but less dramatic, shifts occurred in the legitimacy measures for criminal and constitutional law but little effect was evidenced for these latter law areas in sanctioning preference. It seems that once people learn something is against the law, they are more likely to think it should be (see also Podgorecki, 1973) particularly for civil law matters. It also appears that in civil law areas people may believe some form of sanction is in order where they previously did not just because they learn of the existence of an applicable civil law norm.

This prompts us to conclude that while other students (Evan, 1962; Zimring and Hawkins, 1971) have speculated about the conditions under which law is successful in implementing social change, they have overlooked a basic variable—the distinction between types of law suggested by Durkheim. Our data indicate that the basic divisions of law are not arbitrary but represent real differences in normative orientations that may either catalyze or inhibit attitude change.

NOTES

1. While other students have discussed the "educative" (Andaneas, 1971) or "socializing" (Zimring and Hawkins, 1971) effects of the criminal law's sanctions, the declaratory argument more narrowly focuses only on attitude change due to the mere declaration or removal of the law absent any other circumstances. No threat of punishment or probability of enforcement, no preexisting custom or behavioral compliance, no courtroom drama or public sanctioning are necessarily entailed within the purview of the declaratory argument.

2. Two more differences between the pretest and posttest means are statistically significant if a more lenient decision rule of .01 is employed.

3. Unfortunately, this was the only item which yielded a significant shift for the control sample (suggesting a contesting effect) when moral condemnation was remeasured on Part II of the questionnaire. However, the treatment group evidenced significant change over and above that shown by the control group. For further discussion, see Lanza-Kaduce (1978).

4. This shift occurred among those whose knowledge perceptions were not correct at the pretest. Although we expected the shift in legitimacy for civil law matters that resulted among those whose original legal knowledge perceptions were incorrect, we failed to anticipate that this would occur in criminal and constitutional areas of law as well. Interestingly, changes in legitimacy attributions for five of the six items varied significantly by whether people's knowledge perceptions were confirmed or contradicted. The only other attitude changes that showed significant differences by amount of prior knowledge of the law were sanctioning preferences for both civil law examples. For other normative attitudes and other items, the mere declaration of the legal position evidently can operate either by reinforcing and confirming accurate knowledge perceptions or by correcting mistaken notions about the law, because no change differences by level of prior knowledge were found in these instances.

Peter C. Yeager
Yale University

Marshall B. Clinard
University of Wisconsin—Madison

4

REGULATING CORPORATE BEHAVIOR
A Case Study

This essay is a preliminary report on the development of regulation and enforcement in one relatively recently defined area of corporate criminality: industrial water pollution. This case study is part of a larger ongoing investigation into the nature and distribution of the illegal behavior of the nation's 582 largest industrial, wholesale, retail, and service corporations and their 101 largest subsidiaries during 1975 and 1976.[1]

The control of industrial water pollution has been selected for intensive analysis because it involves a contemporary example of the imposition of the federal criminal sanction on behavior which industrial firms had traditionally considered a necessary concomitant of economic prosperity and growth. The application of the criminal law in this area reflects the drastic shift in environmental values which occurred during the last decade, and permits the analysis of factors which impinge on the social control of corporate behavior amidst evolving climates of opinion.

The use of criminal penalties for water pollution reached a high point when, on October 5, 1976, the federal government fined the Allied Chemical Corporation $13.24 million for its discharges of the pesticide Kepone into Virginia's

James River.[2] Not only was this single assessment greater than the total fines and penalties imposed in *all* Environmental Protection Agency (EPA)-initiated cases (covering water, pesticides, and air pollution) which had been concluded through September 1976 (see EPA, 1977: 1), but merely seven years earlier fines were not even part of the federal government's general response to the increasingly threatening environmental degradation due to water pollution. Indeed, the federal presence in this area of regulatory control is itself of relatively recent origin; legislation to protect water quality for such uses as swimming and fishing was not passed until after World War II.[3] Furthermore, enforcement of water pollution regulations between 1948 and 1970 was very weak and—predictably—ineffectual (Wenner, 1974; Fallows, 1971; Zwick and Benstock, 1971). With the introduction of the criminal sanction and other measures in the early 1970s, the federal government significantly stiffened its stance against industrial water pollution.

The investigation of such developments in legislation, violation, and enforcement is significant to criminology in a number of respects. First, as the present authors have recently suggested (Clinard and Yeager, 1978), the study of corporate criminality provides a theoretical corrective to a criminology heretofore largely focused on individual crimes of violence and theft, with a consequent overconcentration on poverty as an explanation of crime. Secondly, Stone (1977: 4) has noted that as large corporations take over ever greater proportions of the nation's activities, "an increasing share of misconduct will originate in the corporate sector." Not only are many citizens in the aggregate victimized by such misconduct (e.g., price-fixing, polluting, unfair labor practices, dangerously designed and constructed products), but in recent years more types of corporate illegalities have been deemed criminal by the Congress (e.g., polluting, making foreign payoffs), thereby placing more of such activity squarely within the purview of criminology. Finally, the study of corporate criminality focuses attention on the fundamentally political nature of the process of social control which links law creation, infraction, and enforcement; the understanding of that process is essential to the development of an adequate theoretical view of crime.[4] One cannot, in fact, make sense of enforcement patterns and trends without analyzing the historical development of legislation and regulatory policy which has evolved under particular social and political conditions. The character of the legislation limits and determines the character of violation and enforcement, and at many points the process of social control bears the impress of negotiations between powerfully situated corporations, their government regulators, and other interest groups.

The purpose of this essay is to review the developments in legislation and policy affecting industrial water pollution, and to connect these developments to enforcement outcomes, emphasizing throughout the political and organizational factors which in great part determine the character of control. After a brief consideration of some more general considerations concerning government regulation of business, the discussion will turn to the legislative history and enforcement trends.

REGULATING BUSINESS: SELECTED ISSUES

Over the years there have been a number of studies and analyses of government regulation of business which can provide a framework for comparison for the present study. In general, these studies have been critical of the federal government's efforts to control business behavior in the public interest, often arguing that such regulation is at best weak or sporadic, or at worst in the interests of the regulated rather than in the interest of the public weal (cf., the Nader Reports by Turner, 1970; Fellmeth, 1970; Green, 1972, on the Food and Drug Administration, the

Interstate Commerce Commission and the Department of Justice/Federal Trade Commission, respectively). One of the more noted explanations given for considerable regulatory failure is that some agencies become "captured" by the powerful business interests they ostensibly control. Such "capture" may occur through a process of cooptation in which the agency, in order to achieve a stable working environment and avert political threats to its existence, procedurally incorporates some of the interests of the regulated into its decision-making machinery (cf., Selznick, 1966; Neuman, 1977: 11-12). Under these circumstances, policy outcomes—including those in enforcement—may often favor strong private interests as against the public interest in equity, deterrence, and so on.

Another, but related, theme in the literature is that government regulation may produce more symbolic than tangible outcomes (Edelman, 1964), suggesting that the actual purpose of such regulation is to channel political discontent and allay public anxiety while leaving fundamentally undisturbed the distributions of power and wealth in society (Andersen et al., 1976).[5] Again, the implication is that strict regulation in the public interest, as proclaimed in political pronouncements, may be vitiated behind a facade of government activity. Edelman (1964: 37) has argued that this may occur through administrative policy, budgetary starvation, "or other little publicized means."

Such considerations should sensitize the researcher to a variety of factors which may influence regulatory policy outcomes, including enforcement activities. Critical points in the regulatory process are those which involve *negotiation* between the parties involved, and those at which *discretion* must be exercised by the regulators. The complex administrative procedures which attend much regulation afford a number of points of access at which private sector interests—corporate and others—may seek to inject their viewpoints and influence policy. While all sides to a dispute may formally have equal access, Edelman (1964: 51) has maintained that the more organized interests—and traditionally these have often been business interests—tend to receive disproportionately favorable outcomes. Similarly, there are often many points at which the regulatory authorities must use discretion in enforcing the laws. Rosenbaum (1977: 101) notes that discretionary administrative policy-making results when the Congress enacts legislation in broad outline, "leaving administrators with the responsibility of filling in the details and eliminating the vagaries as their more technical training dictates." As pollution control involves technical questions concerning manufacturing processes, abatement technology, pollution loads, and the like, legislation in this area leaves considerable policy-making in the hands of administrators. Discretionary decision-making may also result in policy bias favoring strong, organized interests.

GROWTH OF THE FEDERAL PRESENCE:
1890-1970

The origins of a federal regulatory presence in water pollution control can be traced to the 1890s, when a series of laws culminated in the River and Harbor Act of 1899 (also known as the Refuse Act), a criminal statute which provided a fine of between $500 and $2,500 and/or imprisonment of thirty days to a year for discharges which impeded or obstructed navigation. While this law could technically be interpreted as applicable to industrial discharges of any pollutants into navigable waters (see next section), until 1970 the statute was used only to prosecute those dischargers who created impediments to navigation or anchorage (Glenn, 1973: 840). Federal attempts to regulate in any fashion general industrial discharges were almost fifty years away.

The first such attempt was embodied in the Federal Water Pollution Control Act (FWPCA) of 1948. With this establishment of a federal foothold in what had previously been a preserve of the states, federal regulation began a line of development marked by legislative and administrative changes, both of which were reflected in enforcement trends.[6]

Development of the Enforcement Conference

The terms of the 1948 act reflected state and local opposition to federal intrusion (Wenner, 1974: 266), emphasizing research and technical assistance to the states (which few states' rights proponents would oppose), and providing a multistage enforcement mechanism so cumbersome and fraught with delay that "the House Appropriations Committee denied fiscal 1956 funds to the Public Health Service for enforcement, on the grounds that the existing law was 'almost unenforceable'" (Davies and Davies, 1975: 29). The law applied only to pollution of interstate waters which endangered "the health or welfare of persons in a State other than that in which the discharge originates." In cases of such pollution, the government was authorized to notify the polluter and responsible state agency and recommend "reasonable and equitable" abatement measures. If compliance was not forthcoming after a "reasonable time," a second notification was authorized, followed by a public hearing if noncompliance again continued. Finally, if still no action was taken, the government *could* request the U.S. Attorney General to bring suit in federal court, but with the critical proviso that it could do so only with the permission of the agency or state which had presumably chosen not to act forcibly on its own.

The FWPCA amendments of 1956 improved somewhat on the enforcement structure, but left intact an emphasis on negotiation, state prerogative, and discretion. This law substituted a three-part enforcement mechanism for cases of interstate pollution: a conference of state and federal agencies, polluters and antipollution spokespersons; a public hearing if recommended abatement action was not taken (allowing at least six months for such action); and if still no action (and at least another six months), a request that the U.S. Attorney General bring suit, but only with the consent of the state water pollution control agency in the polluter's state or at the written request of the state endangered by the pollution. For the next fourteen years, this procedure formed the basic structure of federal enforcement.[7]

Several points may be made about the use of the conference mechanism. First, there were established many critical points of discretion, concerning both matters of procedure and definition. Such terms as "reasonable time" and "equitable" abatement recommendations have no adequate referents, leaving central determinations to the law's administrators. Furthermore, the FWPCA enjoined federal courts hearing water cases to give "due consideration to the practicability and to the physical and economic feasibility of securing abatement of any pollution proved." Such a directive provided an ultimate defense for polluters who could demonstrate economic necessity in court (Wenner, 1974: 275).

Second, the conference procedure indicated an emphasis on negotiation and mutual agreement rather than coercion and stiff law enforcement. The issues were defined as technical rather than legal, as problems to be solved by experts rather than by court order. And although antipollution forces could be heard at the conferences, according to Wenner (1974: 282) such spokesmen tended to be given merely formal recognition by the negotiators, who soon returned to discussing technical and economic considerations. The direction of any bias in the system is apparent.

Third, the enforcement process left critical prerogative and initiative in the hands of the states, reflecting the federal position that the states were primarily responsible for enforcing pollution laws. In thus respecting the political pressure for states' rights, the federal government was abdicating pollution control to jurisdictions many of which had, in general, weak records in this area and which were more vulnerable to the threats (e.g., to move to more accomodating states) and persuasions of industry (cf., Ridgeway, 1970; Wenner, 1972). The intent of the conferences was to publicize the polluting activity and bring the weight of public opinion to bear on both the polluters and the state agencies. However, the overriding emphasis on negotiation and cooperation in a context of discretionary decision-making on technical and economic issues, and insulated from meaningful public participation, could be expected to short-cut significant pressures to abate pollution.

Finally, federal initiative was limited to *inter*state waters, which have been estimated to include only 14% of the nation's rivers and streams (Zwick and Benstock, 1971: 294). Though the 1961 FWPCA Amendments included navigable intrastate waters, in general the federal government could not intervene in such cases without the request of the state's governor. Zwick and Benstock (1971: 231) suggest that in part due to the political pressure corporations can muster at the state level, eight of the eleven enforcement conferences initiated by governors for intrastate pollution were called during the governor's final year in office, in at least some cases to assure that "the enmity his request would create could no longer jeopardize the Governor's other programs."

Organizational Factors

Besides the terms of the legislation the administration of the law affects its utility. Over the thirty-year history of the FWPCA responsibility for enforcement has rested in four different agencies or departments (Federal Security Agency, HEW, Interior, EPA) and at least five different administrative structures. Not only can such reorganizations involve disruption of program continuity and loss of expertise (Wenner, 1974: 265), but the location of a regulatory program is an important political choice which can affect the direction and tenor of enforcement. The administration of the 1948 act, for example, was given to the Public Health Service (PHS) of the Federal Security Agency (the predecessor agency to HEW), reflecting the traditional public and congressional concern for clean water for human consumption; general resource conservation had not yet asserted itself in national priorities. One consequence, Ridgeway (1970: 53-54) has argued, is that as the threat of waterborne disease declined, PHS doctors involved began to side with state and local health doctors (responsible for water pollution in many jurisdictions) who had lost some interest in pollution control, thereby pitting PHS doctors against attorneys in the federal agency's enforcement section. Such internal disagreement can be expected only to impede enforcement. Another example of administrative effects is provided by the 1966 reorganization which sent water pollution control from HEW to the Department of the Interior. Zwick and Benstock (1971: 126) claim that the move resulted in the virtual retirement of the federal enforcement program for three years. Others (Ridgeway, 1970: 66; Wenner, 1974: 265) have suggested the explanation that pollution control contradicted Interior's primary commitment to the development rather than the conservation of natural resources, a commitment more in line with industrial interests in growth. Such arguments helped to bring about the establishment of the independent Environmental Protection Agency in 1970.

Environment Results

The data on conferences held from 1957 through mid-1972 bear out many of these points.[8] Nationally, sixty conferences were called during the fifteen-year period. Of these, only four proceeded to the hearing stage, and only one to court, when the city of St. Joseph, Missouri was ordered to abate its pollution. Furthermore, rather than proceed directly from conference to hearing, twenty-nine of the first fifty-one conferences called (57%) held multiple sessions or were reconvened (as of February 1971). In these twenty-nine cases the average length of time elapsed between the first and last meetings was four years, approximately the span between the conference and the court consent decree in the St. Joseph case. With negotiation and cooperation the order of the day, federal enforcement was negligible and water quality showed little improvement (Zwick and Benstock, 1971: 191-201).

An Alternative Approach

The inadequacy of these enforcement procedures in part stimulated the passage of the next set of FWPCA amendments, the Water Quality Act of 1965. Under the act the states were to establish water quality standards for their interstate waters by June 30, 1967, the standards to be subject to the approval of the secretary of HEW. Besides establishing a basis for more uniform standards at least for interstate waters, the law provided a more streamlined enforcement alternative, empowering the federal government to take standards' violators to court after having issued a notice of violation and allowing 180 days for compliance. The first notices were not issued until 1969, however, perhaps in part because many states missed the 1967 deadline for establishing standards. By February 1971, twenty states still had only partly approved standards (Zwick and Benstock, 1971: 446-448).

Enforcement activity was stepped up with the establishment of EPA at the end of 1970; by December 1972, EPA had issued 143 notices (Davies and Davies, 1975: 210). However, court cases were vitually nonexistent under this enforcement provision (Wenner, 1974 reports one case: Reserve Mining on Lake Superior), though it should be noted that by the early 1970s the federal government had civil and criminal authority under the Refuse Act of 1899 which it used somewhat more extensively (see next section). The normal procedure again was for federal officials and violators to meet in an informal hearing and reach mutually agreeable solutions. In addition, the majority of notices were issued to municipalities. Nationally, industrial polluters were spared hard enforcement under the 1965 provisions. Zwick and Benstock (1971: 299) have argued that this result was a consequence of powerful political pressures to favor polluters in the context of federal discretion to choose from among enforcement responses.

THE CRIME OF POLLUTION: 1970-1977

Ponderous and ineffective enforcement was not to survive the dramatic increase in public environmental concern which occurred in the late 1960s and early 1970s. National polls indicated that the percentage responding that local water pollution was a serious problem increased from 35% to 74% (89% in large cities) between 1965 and 1970. In addition, a Harris poll in 1971 reported that 41% of the sample chose pollution as a problem requiring congressional action, second only to "state of the economy" (63%), and ahead of crime (18%) [Erskine, 1972].

Called by one writer "the high renaissance of ecological politics" (Rosenbaum, 1977: 6), the years 1968-1972 were marked by precipitous growth in environmental activism on the part of citizen groups, the establishment of the Environmental Protection Agency in 1970, and the passage of the most sweeping amendments ever to the FWPCA in 1972. This groundswell of concern, according to Rosenbaum (1977: 7-8), "caught the American business community by surprise and threw it on the defensive, thereby putting a traditionally formidable sector of opposition to many environmental regulations at a disadvantage that, momentarily, disarmed it politically."

Several factors are commonly offered for the timing of the environmental movement, including environmental crises (e.g., the Santa Barbara oil spill in 1969, the mercury poison scare in Japan), a high standard of living which allowed the U.S. citizenry the "luxury" of considering environmental quality, the experience of popular organizing gained in the Civil Rights movement and the Viet Nam war, protests, and increased ability to detect pollutants and measure their effects. A major additional factor was the serious growth in industrial pollution, both in terms of quantity and quality (Gunningham, 1974: 32). According to the Council on Environmental Quality (1970: 32):

> The more than 300,000 water-using factories in the United States discharge three to four times as much oxygen-demanding wastes as all the sewered population of the United States. Moreover, many of the wastes discharged by industry are toxic. . . . The output of industrial wastes is growing several times faster than the volume of sanitary sewage.

Presently, the major threat to human health from industrial wastes is posed by the estimated 500 new chemicals which are produced yearly in this country, along with the older chemicals and metals used in industrial processes (Davies and Davies, 1975: 13).

It was the combination of agitated public involvement, Congressional disenchantment with hamstrung federal enforcement, and liberal court rulings in the 1960s which led to the "reincarnation" of the 1899 Refuse Act as a statute prohibiting water pollution in 1970. A Supreme Court decision in 1966 (U.S. versus Standard Oil Co.) broadly interpreted the act's prohibition against the discharge of "any refuse matter of any kind or description whatever" to include discharges of "pollutants." Given this precedent, and under increasing congressional pressure to enforce the act vigorously against industrial polluters, the Corps of Engineers (which had previously enforced the act only as a means of protecting navigation) announced a policy of full enforcement in July 1970.

Inasmuch as only 415 of the approximately 40,000 industrial plants discharging into navigable waters had obtained Refuse Act permits between 1899 and 1970, this interpretation and policy decision, write Zwick and Benstock (1971: 286) meant that 99% of these dischargers in 1970 were "committing a crime when they dump anything but pure water into our navigable waterways."

The policy of "full enforcement," however, did not materialize. Through March 1971, the federal government had used the Refuse Act to stop continuing pollution against only 28 polluters (Zwick and Benstock, 1971: 288). The scope of the task, of course, was prohibitive. In addition, the Justice Department, which was to prosecute any such cases, took the position that the responsibility for controlling "pollution of a continuing nature from the ordinary operations of manufacturing plants" rested with the Interior Department under the FWPCA, and with the states; Justice policy was to use the act "to punish or prevent significant discharges, which are either accidental or infrequent, but which are not of a continuing nature."[9] Thus, despite an increasingly favorable popular climate for the criminal prosecution of industrial polluters, the Justice Department chose to defer to the weak and susceptible (to corporate influence) enforcement apparatuses of the FWPCA and state agencies.

This result is understandable from an organizational standpoint in at least two respects. First, full enforcement under the law was not a reasonable goal given the nature and immensity of the task and the limited resources of a government department charged with enforcing all federal statutes. Second, given the investment in water quality standards and pollution control—however ineffective—made by the Federal Water Quality Administration (Department of Interior), it is unlikely that it would be willing to sacrifice to another agency a critical component of its justification for existence (i.e., the enforcement/compliance task). Bureaucratic tendencies to jealously protect institutional domains (Becquai, 1977) may even lead to noncooperation between federal departments, as indicated in a Justice Department spokesman's complaint that the Interior Department had refused to supply any information or technical advice to Justice for cases it had chosen to prosecute. The Interior Department had communicated an unwillingness to criminally prosecute otherwise respectable business firms (Ridgeway, 1970: 163-166), reflecting a continuing ambivalency in the federal government concerning the nature of pollution violations.

Rather than use the Refuse Act as a primary enforcement tool, the federal government instead chose to make it the basis for a federal permit program established December 1970 by executive order of the president. The basic idea behind the program was to issue discharge control permits to industrial plants, violations of permit conditions constituting violations of the Refuse Act. The plan had the advantages not only of the more efficient enforcement mechanism, but also was applied—as per the law—to intrastate navigable waters as well as to interstate waters. It had the disadvantage, however, of relying on the individual states' determinations as to whether discharges violated state standards on intrastate waters—standards which could be lower than federally approved interstate standards (Zwick and Benstock, 1971: 293).

Enforcement under the Refuse Act permit program reflected EPA's general policy that litigation was to be used as a last resort, when voluntary compliance could not be negotiated (Glenn, 1973: 848). According to EPA enforcement guidelines for the program, criminal prosecutions were to be reserved generally for cases of isolated or instantaneous discharges which caused serious damage, while civil cases were largely aimed at securing court-ordered abatement requirements rather than prohibiting the offending discharges altogether. The agency, in other words, chose to use litigation more as a prod than as a stick. And while environmentalists may have been dissatisfied with the pace of enforcement, the prosecutions under the act in the early 1970s (see Table 1) established the criminal sanction as one tool in regulating industrial water polluters.

The 1972 Amendments

Several factors account for the radical revision of the enforcement program which occurred in 1972. The Refuse Act permit program was administratively cumbersome, involving four federal agencies and the individual states, and carried prospects for uneven standards. Second, it was recognized that the maximum criminal fine of $2,500 per day of violation would not be a deterrent for many major polluters. Third, considerable media attention and critical analyses of enforcement procedures in this area published by Nader's investigators (Fallows, 1971; Zwick and Benstock, 1971) and others also stimulated congressional action.

The 1972 amendments to the FWPCA call for a national permit program for dischargers based on EPA-established effluent limitation guidelines for various industry groups. The permits spell out construction schedules for abatement equipment and the amounts of specified pollutants a plant may discharge. The act states that by July 1, 1977, all industrial plants were to achieve that level of discharge which reflects "the application of the best practicable control technology currently available," and by July 1, 1983, that level reflecting the use of "the best available technology economically achievable." The law asserts that "it is the national goal that the discharge of pollutants into the navigable waters be eliminated by 1985." Furthermore, the act provides significantly strengthened penalties for violation: up to $10,000 per day of violation in civil penalties, and up to $25,000 a day and a year in prison ($50,000 and two years for recidivists) in criminal penalties. Finally, the act provided for citizen civil suits against violators of the law, including EPA in cases of agency failure to carry out nondiscretionary duties.

TABLE 1
Water Enforcement Actions Initiated by EPA[a]

	REFUSE ACT (Referrals to Justice)			FWPCA			
	CIVIL	CRIMINAL	Failure to Apply for Permits	ADMINISTRATIVE ORDERS	NOTICES OF VIOLATION	REFERRALS TO JUSTICE [b]	TOTAL
July, 1971[c] Dec., 1972	106	169	96	----	143	----	514
1973	11	57		19	---	9 (7)	96
1974	2	22		514	----	38	576
1975	7[e]			751	100	113	971
1976 [d]				863	134	102	1099
1977				1035	295	138	1468

a. Actions taken under Refuse Act and 1972 amendments permit program; does not include oil spill enforcement actions or cases initiated by the Department of Justice. The enforcement actions reflected in the table include municipal as well as industrial dischargers. Except where otherwise noted, data were compiled from EPA Enforcement Reports.

b. Except for the seven criminal referrals in parentheses, the data on which the table is based do not distinguish between criminal civil referrals.

c. Data for this one-and-one-half year period were taken from Davies and Davies (1975: 209); notices of violation are for period December 1970-December 1972.

d. Data for 1976 and 1977 taken from EPA paper ("Recent Developments in Federal Water Pollution Enforcement") presented at ALI-ABA Course of Study: Environmental Law, Washington, D.C., Feb. 9-11, 1978.

e. Data source did not distinguish between civil and criminal referrals.

The assigned task was clearly immense. EPA data (as of February 1978) show 41,000 permit applications from nonmunicipal (largely industrial) dischargers, with 27,500 permits having been processed and issued by EPA or approved states (which administer the permits and enforcement under EPA regulations; twenty-nine states and the Virgin Islands have been approved). Including municipal treatment plants and other dischargers, total applicants numbered 67,500 with almost 50,000 permits issued. In addition, EPA was given the technically complex assignment of determining "best practicable technology" and "best available technology" for the numerous industrial categories being regulated.

The size and nature of the problem, as well as the tight timetables in the legislation, dictated that EPA early establish priorities for implementation and enforcement of its program. The first priority was the establishment of effluent limitations and the issuance of permits, resulting in an enforcement moratorium period for plants during the pendency of acceptable permit applications (Table 1, 1973). As more permits were issued containing compliance deadlines and effluent discharge limits, more of the agency's attention turned to enforcement by 1974, as indicated by the great increase in administrative orders to come into compliance (Table 1). The next year, 1975, referrals to the Justice Department for civil and criminal action under the FWPCA jumped markedly (replacing referrals under the Refuse Act); it can be noted from the data in Table 1, though, that administrative remedies continue to account for the bulk of agency enforcement actions. However, Table 2 indicates that with the passing of July 1, 1977, deadline for firms to have established "best practicable control technology," EPA more than doubled its referrals to Justice over the comparable half-year period a year earlier, underscoring a policy of stronger legal sanctions in cases of violation of the statutory deadline.

TABLE 2
Water Enforcement Actions, July to December, 1976 and 1977

	July-Dec. 1977	July-Dec. 1976
Notices of Violation	151	70
Administrative Orders	392	395
Referrals to Justice	82	40
Totals	625	505

Source: Environmental Protection Agency (1978) ''Recent Developments in Federal Water Pollution Enforcement.'' Presented at ALI-ABA Course of Study: Environmental Law, Washington, D.C., Feb. 9-11.

Ongoing Research—Some Considerations

Unlike earlier regulatory attempts, the 1972 amendments have succeeded in stemming some of the nation's difficult pollution problems (Council on Environmental Quality, 1976: 255-285). EPA's enforcement program, with its emphasis on the approximately 3,700 major business polluters, has played an important role in the agency's achievements. According to EPA data, the agency anticipated that only about 15% of major industrial polluters would violate the 1977 deadline.

In terms of continuing enforcement efforts, however, EPA faces the common regulatory problems of vast oversight responsibility and limited resources with which to carry out its mandate, in terms of technical staff and inspection personnel as well as enforcement resources. Optimal enforcement against all violations is not possible, and the agency must establish priorities. These difficulties are only compounded by the fact that EPA's regulatory program is expected to enforce new financial priorities on industry; traditionally, water was a "free good" for industrial consumption.

Furthermore, EPA faces political pressures from both sides: business and conservationists. The character of enforcement can be expected to reflect the ways in which such influences are incorporated into agency policy and decision-making.

For example, the nature of EPA's responsibilities dictates that the agency engage in negotiation with industry and use discretion. Both industry input and agency discretion pertain in the technically complex problems of defining such terms as "best practicable technology" for industry groups and of constructing compliance schedules for individual plants. The sorts of determinations made at these stages may be reflected in later violation rates across firms and industries. For instance, Alexander (1976: 130) has contended that EPA has increasingly been granting exemptions from and modifications to their requirements for specific plants (Rosenbaum, 1977: 164). Companies so exempted may appear less in enforcement data than firms not exempted. In addition, agency procedure provides for administrative adjudicatory hearings for firms wishing to contest permit conditions imposed on their plants. The distribution of adjudicatory hearings may also be related to subsequent violation rates and distributions.

On the other hand, the period of the late 1960s and the late 1970s has seen a marked increase in the use of the courts by citizen groups to achieve environmental goals. Some of the newer environmental groups, such as the Natural Resources Defense Council (NRDC) and the Environmental Defense Fund, have concentrated largely on litigation as a means of enforcing the terms of legislation (Davies and Davies, 1975: 90). Some suits have been directed at forcing EPA to meet various responsibilities, such as two NRDC suits since 1972 which resulted in orders that the agency establish effluent discharge limits by specified deadlines and for various pollutants. An additional input into agency policy is the aforementioned citizen suit provision of the 1972 amendments. To the extent that activist organizations exercise oversight concerning environmental conditions, EPA decision-making and enforcement may reflect various environmentalist viewpoints.

The present research is an attempt to assess the impact conflicting political pressures may have on violation rates and enforcement response. Combining analyses of internal policy memoranda and legislative documents with statistical analyses of violation and enforcement data, the investigation seeks to study the relationship between policy and enforcement activity, to relate both to the political and economic influences active over time, and to correlate violations and sanctions with characteristics of firms and industries over the period of the permit program for which data are accessible. The analysis will attempt to illuminate the nature and relative influence of the political and economic factors which affect both rates of violation and agency response.

SUMMARY AND CONCLUSIONS

While critical to the development of academic criminology, the study of corporate crime has been relatively undeveloped despite Sutherland's beginnings. This essay has argued, and sought to demonstrate, that such study offers important insights into the nature of the social, political, and organizational forces which influence both the definition of infraction and its social control. Early legislation in the area of water pollution control, while reflecting recognition of a growing social probelm, was deferent to the interests of the business economy to the extent that its enforcement provisions were rendered impotent. Here, control was fundamentally "symbolic." Regulation became a significant enterprise only with the development of a specific constellation of political and environmental factors. However, given the nature of this area of control, with its emphasis on negotiation and discretion, and given the potential political impact of organized interests, the character of regulation may reflect structural biases. More research is needed to investigate such possibilities in numerous areas of corporate regulation. Shifts in the application of sanctions to business enterprises should reveal much of the nature of social control.

NOTES

1. This research is supported by a grant from the Law Enforcement Assistance Administration (LEAA) of the United States Department of Justice (Grant No. 77NI-99-0069). The views expressed herein are the sole responsibility of the authors, and do not necessarily reflect those of LEAA.

2. The court later reduced the fine to $5 million when Allied Chemical donated $8 million to a new, nonprofit corporation which would fund research projects and implement remedial activities to help mitigate Kepone damage. Allied also made a contribution to fund Kepone-related medical research and paid some of the clean-up costs. For additional information on this most noteworthy case see Stone (1977), Kelly (1977) and Reitze and Reitze (1976).

3. Individual states and localities had such legislation prior to the entry of the federal government into the area of general water pollution in 1948 (see Wenner, 1972). Also, the federal government had passed a 1924 law prohibiting oil pollution from ocean-going vessels, though the law proved to be not very effective (see Davies and Davies, 1975: 27).

4. Cressey (1978) has recently decried the trend in criminology away from basic research and toward a technology of crime control; he urges a return to more theoretical concerns with the social conditions under which laws are enacted, broken, and enforced, in order to better approach valid generalizations concerning crime in society. The present authors are in agreement with Cressey on this point. We reiterate the importance of grasping the dynamic interrelationships between lawmaking, violation, and enforcement.

5. To the extent that the regulation of industrial water pollution involves forcing business to bear a portion of the costs, such regulation is redistributive inasmuch as industry previously had been consuming a national resource without cost (see Enloe, 1975: viii, foreword by Martin O. Heisler).

6. Subsequent federal water pollution control legislation has consisted of amendments to the 1948 law; it has been amended seven times: 1956, 1961, 1965, 1966, 1970, 1972, and 1977.

7. The 1961 amendments broadened the scope of the statute by bringing navigable waters (which may be intrastate) under the law's purview. The amendments also did away with the consent provision which had qualified the ability to seek federal court action in cases of interstate pollution endangering citizens of other states, but left the consent proviso in cases of intrastate pollution. The 1965 Act made an additional enforcement mechanism available to federal authorities, as discussed below.

8. For a discussion of conference data, see Wenner (1974: 278-280) and Zwick and Benstock (1971: Appendix A).

9. *Justice Department Guidelines for Litigation Under the Refuse Act*, 1 B.N.A. Environment Reporter—Current Developments 288 (July 17, 1970).

Steven Thomas Seitz
University of Illinois

5

GUNS, POLITICS, AND PUBLIC POLICY

SCIENCE AND POLITICS

Twentieth century America differs greatly from its nineteenth century predecessor, but we seldom reflect on the fundamental causes of these differences. One such cause is modern science. In the nineteenth century scientific knowledge was not particularly specialized, and the available expertise was widely disseminated through modest education and practical experience. Twentieth century science, in contrast, became highly abstract and specialized; its acquisition required intensive education and could not be learned through traditional apprenticeships. While the techniques of nineteenth century science reflected the trial and error of crass empiricism, those of the twentieth century began to reflect an intricate link between abstract theory and sophisticated experimentation (Rosenberg, 1974; Levi-Strauss, 1966).

This transformation of science had enormous implications for society and government. The new science helped create a professional elite clearly distinguished from more ordinary men and women. These professionals understood the forces of nature and the condition of society in ways foreign to the common wisdom, and the technical abstractions of twentieth century knowledge fostered a growing gap between the expertise of professionals and the knowledge of ordinary people. The need to translate professional jargon into common parlance hindered the flow of ideas from experts to the masses, while the arrogance of specialization hampered the flow of ideas from the masses to the experts. In a democratic society where equality was one cornerstone of the public philosophy, this knowledge gap helped to create serious tensions between expertise and numbers in the calculus of power.

America's emerging industrial society brought with it complex social problems and vigorous governmental efforts to address those problems. Professionals were in great demand. In fact, three major eras of the twentieth century mark the political ascendancy of professionals over more ordinary citizens. At the turn of the century, Progressive reformers brought scientific management and expertise into government. Their belief in the virtues of scientific politics cast doubt on the value of democracy and universal suffrage, leading some of them to advocate education tests and poll taxes so that the ignorant might be disenfranchised. After a period of retrenchment during the 1920s, the professional classes gained stature and power under the New Deal. Lawyers, economists, and other social scientists helped elaborate and administer the bold social initiatives of the Roosevelt Administration. World War II further expanded the role of experts in the government, particularly experts from the physical sciences. A brief retrenchment of governmental professionalization followed the war, but cold war tensions, the launching of Sputnik, and growing domestic unrest once again ushered professionals into positions of preeminent power (Hofstadter, 1963).

The influx of professionals into public service during the twentieth century helped to institutionalize the role of expert administration in the United States, even though the average American chose not to bestow upon these experts a social prestige commensurate with their new position. Max Weber argues that bureaucratic experts exercise control on the basis of superior knowledge, and he suggests that nonexperts can exert only a limited degree of control over existing bureaucratic machinery (Weber, 1964: 338-339). Specialized knowledge more and more becomes the foundation of bureaucratic power, thereby increasing the dominance of professionals, and thus creating an inherent conflict between bureaucracy and democracy in the calculus of power (Weber, 1958: 231-235). Historically, this conflict has been most visible in the clash between social scientists and the public. In one of history's minor ironies, for example, Princeton professor Woodrow Wilson campaigned against expert regulation of big business during his 1912 presidential race. And in 1946, a congressman objected to including the social sciences in the National Science Foundation, because no one should have the right to decide what other people ought to do, and he felt that such decisions were the presumptuous pretentions of social scientists.

The growing gap between professional knowledge and the common wisdom created a serious policy problem in twentiety century America (and many other nations, for that matter): the accommodation of expertise to politics (see Seitz, 1978). The Progressive efforts to fuse science with politics might represent an extreme form of this accommodation, particularly in democratic societies, but we can find other examples of this fusion with a more recent vintage. For example, the fusion of science and politics is a plausible description of military and space policy under the Kennedy and Johnson Administrations. In *The Best and the Brightest,* David Halberstam well documents the crucial role of technocrats like Defense Secretary Robert McNamara. And in other areas, such as nuclear energy, we find examples where scientists actually became policy overlords. No better symbol of this ascendancy exists than that of Glen Seaborg, the Nobel Prize winning scientist President Kennedy persuaded to accept the chairmanship of the Atomic Energy Commission. Other less visible examples might include the Army Corp of Engineers, transportation planners, and even urban planners. In each of these examples, critics charge that the professionals have superseded the democratic process.

C. P. Snow calls this fusion of expertise with politics "closed politics": political choices are made by scientific overlords (Snow, 1962). In the strictest sense, closed politics are antithetical to democratic processes. The antagonism between professionalism and democracy might remain latent for a period of time, as it often does during times of social crisis. As social crises abate, as we noted in the course of twentieth century American politics, the tensions reappear on the political agenda. As a result, the extreme forms of closed politics in America periodically are modified. The resulting accommodation of expertise to politics reflects an uneasy balance between the knowledge of professionals and the common wisdom of ordinary men and women. This uneasy balance reflects the second major form of accommodation found in twentieth century American history. Although this level of accommodation gives great weight to the opinions of experts, that expertise is tempered by electoral politics and the demands of competing interest groups. In part, the Carter administration reflects this uneasy balance between professionals and democrats. This appears to be true with respect to military policy, nuclear energy policy, and certain social policies. And in keeping spirit with the times, even urban planners are now taught in their professional training that popular input must be encouraged rather than avoided.

On the opposite extreme of our continuum regarding the accommodation of expertise to politics we find the classic form of open politics. Here the scope and intensity of popular opinion takes absolute precedence over the advice of experts. This arena includes the gut-level issues on which ordinary people refuse to defer to the opinions of professionals. One obvious issue is gay rights; a majority of citizens appear to hold intense policy preferences, and they hardly are swayed by the intricacies of abstract legal arguments or other professional reasoning (see Hofstadter, 1967). On matters such as these, an attentive public stands ready to exercise its democratic initiative at the polls, on referendums, and through other available channels, should policy makers fail to heed the common wisdom. Other victims of such open politics include those criminal justice experts who, in the popular press, often are termed woolly headed criminal coddlers. On such issues, it would appear, the advice of experts falls on deaf ears or, equally embarrassing to the professional, weighs lightly in the calculus of power.

THE GUN CONTROVERSY

Suppose we examine the gun control controversy in light of our discussion of open, balanced, and closed politics. This particular controversy highlights the tension between experts and democrats. In 1975, for example, Alan Otten of the *Wall Street Journal* solemnly declared that, although Senate and House committees usually like to listen to experts, they turn deaf ears to the advocates of handgun control. Otten explained that Congress believed that the National Rifle Association (NRA) and other opponents of gun control could defeat an office-holder supporting gun legislation. The NRA claims that it defeated former Senator Joseph Tydings, former Senator Joseph Clark, and several others (Otten, 1975). However, in 1977 Representative Conyers (Democrat-Michigan), Chairman of the House Subcommittee on Crime, House Judiciary Committee, requested that the General Accounting Office—the research arm of Congress—prepare a report for Congress on handgun control effectiveness. In its report delivered to Congress on February 6, 1978, the General Accounting Office recommended further legislation to restrict the availability of handguns. The Department of Justice supported the GAO recommendations (General Accounting Office, 1978).

A majority of American citizens have supported some form of handgun registration in all major polls taken since 1938. However, the federal government has enacted only two major pieces of legislation in this area, one in 1938 and the other in 1968. Both legislative enactments occurred during times of severe social unrest, the first corresponding to the organized crime violence of the 1930s and the second corresponding to the urban terrorism of the 1960s. However, in times of quiescence, when the majority of citizens appear inattentive to matters of gun control, a minority of highly organized citizens with intense views on gun control govern the course of public policy. The contours of the gun control controversy bear more than a passing resemblance to the cyclical shift in the balance of power between professionals and democrats during the twentieth century, particularly if we note that the periodic ascendancy of professionals follows the mobilization of an otherwise inattentive majority in response to a real or perceived crisis. The Progressives, for example, mobilized support to fight the trusts and corrupt politicians. Franklin Roosevelt mobilized electoral support for bold governmental initiatives in the depressed economic sector. And Kennedy mobilized support for new initiatives in the technological race with the Soviet Union. Given these parallels, suppose we examine the gun control controversy more closely.

Cultural Heritage

One storybook truth about American history holds that the gun helped American heroes settle the West. Although more fable than fact, the tale does illustrate that the implementation of law and formal social control in the West lagged behind the pace of settlement (Kennett and Anderson, 1975: 124). This encouraged the use of guns in personalized law enforcement, and for some time after the extension of more formal mechanisms of social control, people continued to rely on their own devices for securing justice. However, the problem of guns in personalized law enforcement emerged with startling clarity in the Old South after the Civil War. The Carpetbaggers were not particularly interested in securing or maintaining a civil order comparable to the antebellum era, and the freed slaves plus poor whites found themselves in an environment into which they were not economically integrated. While some of these dispossessed people began to leave the Old South, others became little more than scavengers who rendered much of the remaining social order nasty and brutish. The general civil disorder quickly led to the widespread use of guns for equalizing justice and establishing some minimal sense of personal security in an age of enormous turmoil.

Viewed from this perspective, the gun control controversy implies a potential cleavage between cosmopolitan Americans who find little utility in the gun and an older cultural sector that continues to hold the gun in high esteem. The terrors of past social turmoil and past social insecurity still weigh heavily on many descendants of the Old South, and these cultural pockets remain unwilling to trust their lives and property to a government that once failed to provide the civil order sought by their forefathers. Among urban Americans, on the other hand, we find remnants of cultural traditions brought by emigrants from Europe to America. In Europe, the gun had been first and foremost an instrument of the upper social classes, so the lower classes who entered America had little cultural experience with the gun, particularly the handgun. And in a crowded urban environment, the handgun is a greater source of fear than a government's potential failure to maintain the proper social order, save those situations of urban unrest when residents of the metropolis, like the citizens of Detroit, rush to buy handguns for a sense of security and self-protection. But even under these crisis circumstances, urban people have been willing to register their arms, so long as governments actively enforce the same laws against those who appear to be the source of urban terror (Kennett and Anderson, 1975: 253-254). Registration, as Milton Friedman points out, might assist governments in keeping firearms out of the hands of those who are likely to use them for criminal purposes, and after the criminal event has occurred, it might assist governments in finding out who had access to firearms used in the crime (Friedman, 1962: 145).

A controversy deeply seated in cultural heritage cannot be solved by the advice of experts, because the relative effectiveness of gun control legislation, even if conclusively demonstrated, cannot compensate for the sense of fear and distrust generated by historical events like Reconstruction and subsequently amplified by myths and common wisdom passed from generation to generation. The typical professional often has little empathy for such cultural pockets, partly because such common wisdom is foreign to the professional's image of society and state, and partly because expert knowledge derives from an analysis of facts and figures that are less encumbered by family and other social forces that mold personalities and perpetuate beliefs across generations. Stated differently, the professional is more likely to think in terms of probabilities, while the ordinary men and women from such cultural pockets are more likely to construct the issue in terms of possibilities, the relative improbabilities notwithstanding. If this cultural heritage argument has some merit, then we have one potential explanation why some ordinary people prefer to keep the gun control issue in the domain of open politics, rather than deferring to the judgment of professionals.

The National Rifle Association

On March 21, 1978, the U.S. Treasury Departments' Bureau of Alcohol, Tobacco, and Firearms (AFT) issued a proposed set of updated rules regarding the regulation of firearms. The proposed rules would require that all guns manufactured in the United States bear a serial number, that gun manufacturers, importers, and dealers would submit quarterly reports on the sale and disposition of firearms, that gun dealers and others involved in firearms transactions would report theft or loss of any firearms within twenty-four hours, but that the names and addresses of individual purchasers would not be reported. Consistent with its past procedures, the National Rifle Association misrepresented the implications of these proposed regulations to its vast constituency, and the NRA mobilized a mass mailing effort that produced 300,000 letters against the ATF rules. In addition, the NRA instructed its members to write to congressmen on the House Appropriations Committee, demanding that the committee eliminate funding for the implementation of the proposed rules. Not only did the House Appropriations Committee cut funds for the new rules' implementation, but also the committee explicitly forbade ATF from initiating controversial or sensitive programs without a clear legislative mandate.

The House Appropriations Committee's action was rather stern, given the modest nature of the proposed change of rules, and given the fact that the rules did not directly affect gun consumers. Further, administrative agencies often engage in such policy elaboration, and Congress has been generally tolerant of this quasi-policy function exercised by the federal bureaucracy. In addition, the courts have enforced the need for administrative procedures guaranteeing some hearing for the impacted groups, and ATF had held a number of hearings on its proposed changes. In short, the House Appropriations Committee's response to ATF's proposals well might support the NRA's claims regarding its legislative effectiveness. If the NRA claims are valid, then we have another potential explanation why the gun control issue remains in the domain of open politics.

The Professionals

As is often the case with the federal bureaucracy, the NRA and other progun lobbyists could not keep ATF from putting the revised rules on the political agenda. In part, of course, this reflects the bureau's vested interests in the legislative mandates of 1938 and 1968. In terms of simple efficiency and effectiveness, ATF could better perform its previous legislative mandate with the revised rules it sought to implement. In addition, the ATF proposals were consistent with the spirit of the GAO report delivered to Congress in February; its proposals were consistent with the Justice Department's position that further regulation was necessary; and, the bureau did receive the support of several special interest groups favoring stricter regulation of firearms. In this bureaucratic age, it should not be surprising that governmental agencies seek more closure in the policy arenas that they are required to administer. Stated a different way, the general trend of bureaucratic policy is away from open politics and toward either balanced or closed politics. If this assessment appears reasonable, then we have one potential explanation why the NRA and its associated lobbies failed to keep the gun control matter off the political agenda in 1978. In a sense, the NRA had to expand the scope of conflict into the halls of Congress, precisely because its mass mailing effort and public testimony did not persuade ATF to rescind the proposed rule changes. Unlike the federal agencies, Congress was more responsive to the demands for an open politics in the gun control controversy, as might befit an institution of democratic representation. Without congressional intervention, ATF might have shifted the gun control issue into an arena that established some balance between professional opinion and intense public opinion mobilized by the progun lobbyists, especially given the fact that the public so mobilized constitutes only an intensely vocal minority of the citizenry.

It is against this background that we must assess Representative McClory's (Republican-Illinois) motion to reinstate funding of the ATF proposals and to delete the House Appropriation Committee's language that forbade ATF from implementing the new rules. This motion was made on June 7, 1978, just six days after the House Appropriations Committee took its action against ATF. The motion did not give the NRA time to mobilize a mass mailing campaign against members of the House, although the NRA's threat of retribution at the polls still might hold House members in line. In light of past gun control controversies, the McClory motion did not appear politically shrewd. No assassinations or urban terrorism had mobilized the otherwise inattentive majority of citizens during the Ninety-fifth Congress, several congressmen still faced stiff primary elections where the volatile progun vote might spell electoral defeat, and all the congressmen faced potentially hostile gun proponents in the general elections less than five months away. In light of existing political realities, McClory's motion would be futile.

It is clear, however, that the House vote on McClory's motion involved an issue far deeper than the modest changes proposed by ATF, particularly given the fact that the new rules would have no direct impact on ordinary citizens. The language inserted into the bill by the House Appropriations Committee made it virtually certain that, vis-à-vis ATF, the gun control matter would remain solely in the domain of open politics. McClory's motion, on the other hand, would allow part of the gun controversy to shift from the electoral arena into the bureaucratic arena. A vote for McClory's motion would help shift the gun controversy from the open politics dominated by the NRA into a more balanced accommodation of public hysteria to questions of effectiveness and efficiency.

SOME EMPIRICAL HYPOTHESES

The June 7, 1978 vote on McClory's motion provides us with an opportunity to examine more closely the arguments presented in the previous section. The cultural heritage argument, for example, suggests that the Old South and perhaps parts of the West will stand in opposition to the more cosmopolitan areas of the Northeast, Midwest, and far West. Suppose we grant the assumption that congressmen do represent their constituents on matters of fundamental cultural importance, and suppose, in light of our cultural heritage discussion, that gun control is one such fundamental issue; then we should expect to find strong regional and socioeconomic differences between the constituencies of those representatives supporting the McClory motion and those representatives opposing the McClory motion.

The cultural heritage argument also suggests an ideological schism between those who believe in the beneficient influence of government and those who fear or distrust the powers of government. In particular, we expect that those representatives voting for McClory's motion more likely are liberal in the sense that they favor paternalistic intervention in social matters and often justify it in terms of the enlightened interests of their constituents. Those representatives opposing McClory's motion, on the other hand, should be more conservative in the sense of favoring states' rights, minimal governmental intervention, or the status quo, and often justify it in terms of the potential evils of big government and its insensitivities to common wisdom and the ethic of self-help.

By its own claims, much of the NRA's strength rests upon its ability to defeat congressmen at the polls, and on its ability to mobilize quickly its vast constituency for mass mailing campaigns. If we assume that a congressman's perception of his electoral coalition bears some minimal resemblance to the objective vote returns at election time, then we should expect that congressmen from marginal districts are more likely to oppose gun control regulations, because a campaign against them by the NRA might spell electoral defeat. Based on the NRA's first claim, therefore, we expect that congressmen from safe districts are more likely to support McClory's motion than are congressmen from marginal districts.

The NRA also claims major success in its mass mailing campaigns, arguing that it brings direct constituent pressure on the decision-making of congressmen. As proponents of such campaigns see the issue, letter writing as a form of citizen participation is one essential ingredient of participatory democracy. It is, in short, one device for keeping politics open. Controls on mass solicitations, on the other hand, particularly the registration of those soliciting mass mailings, implies some effort to gauge the spontaneity of mass mailings and thus partly offset the supposed political impact of such campaigns. Given our theoretical expectation that gun control proponents might favor a shift from open politics in the gun control controversy, and given the NRA's assertions regarding the effectiveness of its mass mailing solicitations on congressional voting, we should expect to find that gun control proponents more likely favor the registration of such solicitations than would opponents of gun legislation.

Finally, we have argued that the McClory motion involved a procedural issue far more important than the modest rules proposed by ATF. That issue centers on the degree to which the gun control controversy might be shifted into the bureaucratic arena and hence into a more balanced accommodation of public hysteria and the more sedate questions of gun control effectiveness and gun control efficiency. Our argument suggests that the gun control controversy is part of a larger syndrome of conflicts over the proper locus of policy-making and policy-elaboration along a continuum from open to closed politics. Other issues falling into this larger syndrome might include civil rights for prison inmates, the civil rights of homosexuals, and legal services for the poor. And as the 1946 debate over the inclusion of the social sciences under the National Science Foundation illustrates, this larger syndrome should reflect a conflict between the proper role of professional knowledge versus common wisdom in the political process, with the advocates of a balanced or closed politics favoring the support and use of professional knowledge and with the advocates of open politics opposing the support and use of such professional knowledge over the common wisdom.

SOME EMPIRICAL TESTS

Our first hypothesis suggests strong regional and socio-economic differences between the constituencies of those representatives supporting the McClory motion and those representatives opposing the McClory motion. Of the 435 representatives in the House, 400 either voted on the McClory motion, were paired on the vote, or announced their position on the matter. Of these, 83 favored McClory's motion to restore funding and delete the restrictive language regarding the ATF's proposed rules, while 317 were opposed to McClory's motion. Based on a standard difference of means test, our findings strongly confirm the expectations derived from the cultural heritage argument. Those results are summarized in Table 1.

Table 2 summarizes the regional distribution of constituencies whose representatives opposed or favored the McClory motion. Our expectations regarding the Old South are strongly confirmed.

From the cultural heritage argument we also derived the hypothesis that supporters of McClory's motion would be more liberal than opponents of that motion. By liberal we mean support for federal intervention in social problems, and by conservative we mean support for the ethic of self-help, states' rights, or the status quo. Our measures of these ideological schisms derive from the yearly ratings of congressmen's voting records issued by various special interest groups. The data compare the ratings of congressmen in the first session of the Ninety-fifth Congress as issued by the Americans for Democratic Action, the United States Chamber of Commerce, and the Americans for Constitutional Action. The first group is well noted for its liberal policy preferences, and its members generally support federal intervention in social problems. The remaining two groups are conservative, with the Chamber of Commerce reflecting a modified laissez-faire attitude common among contemporary American businessmen, and with the Ameri-

TABLE 1

Constituency Differences Between Representatives Favoring
McClory's Motion and Representatives Opposing
McClory's Motion on June 7, 1978

	Average Constituency: Opposition	Average Constituency: Supporters	Statistical Significance: Difference of Means
% Urban	68.2%	92.5%	.000
% Parents Born in USA	86.4%	73.5%	.000
% College Educated	10.0%	12.8%	.000
% Employed in Professions	14.1%	16.5%	.000
% of Population Living in Central Cities of SMSA's	26.3%	50.5%	.000

Source: U.S. Department of Commerce (1973) **Congressional District Data Book.**
Washington, DC: U.S. Government Printing Office.

cans for Constitutional Action generally supporting states'
rights and status quo policies. The hypothesis, confirmed by
the data, suggests that supporters of McClory's motion
should have higher ADA ratings (supporters: 74.5% versus
opponents: 32.2%), while opponents of McClory's motion
should have higher CCUS and ACA ratings, respectively
(opponents: 58.9% and 51.3% versus supporters: 20.1%
and 13.7%).[1]

Our third hypothesis suggests that congressmen from
marginal districts are more likely to oppose McClory's
motion, given the NRA's potential threat at election time.
If we grant the assumption that a congressman's perception
of his home district's electoral coalition bears some minimal
relation to the actual results in the last general election,
then a simple test of this hypothesis compares the average
percentage of the vote gained by those opposing McClory's
motion with the average percentage of the vote gained by
those supporting McClory's motion. We expect a smaller
margin of victory among the opponents of McClory's motion,
and the data confirm this expectation. Those opposing
McClory's motion earned an average 67.1% of the electoral

TABLE 2

Regional Distribution of the Constituencies Whose Representatives
Opposed the McClory Motion and Whose Representatives
Favored the McClory Motion on June 7, 1978

	% of the Districts Whose Representatives Opposed McClory's Motion	% of the Districts Whose Representatives Favored McClory's Motion	Significance of the Difference in Proportions
New England	4.8%	12.1%	.003
Middle Atlantic	16.4%	24.1%	.105
East Central	18.9%	26.5%	.129
West Central	9.2%	4.8%	.203
South	27.4%	6.0%	.000
Border	8.8%	3.6%	.114
Mountain	4.4%	2.4%	.407
Pacific	10.7%	19.3%	.036
External (Hawaii and Alaska)	.3%	1.2%	.308

Source: U.S. Department of Commerce (1973) **Congressional District Data Book**.
Washington, DC: U.S. Government Printing Office.

vote in the preceding general election, while those supporting McClory's motion earned an average 70.9% of the vote, a difference significant at .027.[2]

The fourth hypothesis indicates that gun control proponents more likely favor the regulation of mass mailing solicitations than would the opponents of gun legislation. On april 19, 1978 the House of Representatives considered a motion that would require the registration of lobbying solicitations designed to bring constituent pressure on a representative or senator. This vote occurred during the period when the NRA began its mass mailing campaign against ATF and the House Appropriations Committee. The amendment offered by Representative Flowers (Democrat-Alabama) would require the registration of mass mailing solicitations that were paid for by the requesting organization or its affiliate, if the registered lobby spent more than $2,500 per quarter and directed its solicitations at 500 or more people, or twenty-five or more employees, or twelve or more affiliates. The lobby would have to report the solicitation, a description of the issue, the means of solicitation, and the names of people retained to make the solicitation. Supporters of the amendment cited the millions of letters generated through computerized mass solicitations, while opponents of the amendment argued that it invaded the privilege of citizens to petition their government. The amendment passed the House on a vote of 245 in favor, 161 opposed.

We expect to find a larger percentage of those favoring McClory's amendment also voting in favor of the lobby disclosure amendment, while a smaller percentage of those opposing the McClory amendment should vote in favor of the lobby disclosure amendment. Of those opposing McClory's motion 56.4% voted for the disclosure amendment, compared to 66.3% of those supporting the McClory motion. Although the percentages fall in the predicted direction, the difference of means is significant only at the .099 level. The statistics reveal a large amount of variation in the voting among both supporters and opponents of McClory's motion. In part, this variation reflects the diversity of groups using mass mailing techniques, ranging from the NRA to organized labor, various consumer groups, and organized business groups. Common Cause, for example, spends about 70% of its budget on mass mailing solicitations. While the strongly favorable vote on this amendment reflects, at least in part, the enormous burden computerized solicitations place on the congressman's office in answering constituency correspondence, the variation among those supporting and opposing McClory's motion might well reflect a growing insensitivity on the part of congressmen to mass mailings in general. Even the congressmen use computerized responses when answering constitutency mail. In any event, the central tendencies of this data are consistent with the hypothesis, but the significance levels do not permit unequivocal confirmation of the hypothesis.

The fifth hypothesis holds that the gun control controversy is part of a larger syndrome juxtaposing the forces favoring open politics against the forces favoring either a balanced or closed politics. To test this matter within the House of Representatives, we shall examine all the relevant nonredundant votes on criminal justice matters taken in the Ninety-fifth Congress, plus one vote on the funding of biological, behavioral, and social sciences research under the National Science Foundation. We include the NSF vote because antagonism toward the development and use of such expertise historically has emerged regarding the inclusion of social sciences in the National Science Foundation. As noted earlier, the advocates of open politics believe that most people might be considered social scientists, and that ordinary men and women do not want certified professionals from these disciplines telling them what to do.

All told, we have eight votes, including the McClory vote. The eight votes are described in chronological order. In late June 1977 the House adopted an amendment, 230 to 133, prohibiting the Legal Services Corporation from providing legal assistance in cases arising from disputes over homosexuality or gay rights. In September 1977 the House passed a bill, 192 to 173, that established a federal program to reimburse up to 25% of awards paid by states to cover victim compensations for medical expenses and loss of pay as a result of violent crime. In early December 1977 the House adopted, 236 to 110, the conference report authorizing funding for the Legal Services Corporation so that it might provide legal services for the poor. In mid-March 1978 the House passed a resolution providing $2.5 million for the House Select Committee on Assassinations for the remainder of the Ninety-fifth Congress. In mid-April 1978 the House rejected, 174 to 229, an amendment that would reduce by $6 million the fiscal 1979 authorization for biological, behavioral, and social science programs under the

National Science Foundation. In early May 1978 the House adopted an amendment, 227 to 132, that would delete prisons and other correctional facilities from coverage under a bill extending civil rights to institutionalized persons, thus preventing the attorney general from filing suits when such rights violations were found. (A later amendment with considerably fewer congressmen voting reversed this decision.) In late May 1978 the House rejected a motion, 201 to 205, that would suspend the rules and pass a bill to establish a spouse abuse program and authorize its funding. Finally, as noted earlier, the McClory motion was offered on June 7, 1978.

A factor analysis of these eight votes revealed only one underlying dimension, and in all eight cases the voting patterns correlate with the latent dimension as we might expect if the dimension tapped a syndrome of accommodations of expertise with common wisdom, ranging from open politics through balanced politics to closed politics.[3] Suppose we examine the factor scores derived from this analysis in a multivariate stepwise regression using all the variables implicated in the first four hypotheses.[4] This analysis provides a comparative assessment of the first four arguments as they relate to the open/closed politics dimension suggested in hypothesis five. Three variables account for 73% of the variation in factor scores derived from the latent dimension: ADA rating (beta = .818, sig. = .000), percentage of the constituency in urban areas (beta = .091, sig. = .001), and the size of a congressman's electoral victory in 1976 (beta = .066, sig. = .010). In short, all but the mass mailing hypothesis contribute to an explanation of the latent dimension.

To examine how well we can explain the gun control vote, we use a multivariate procedure called discriminant analysis, which allows us to use a dichotomous dependent variable (the gun vote) and several interval-level variables. Again, we use a stepwise procedure, allowing any of the variables discussed in hypotheses one through four to enter the equation, provided they meet rigorous statistical inclusion levels.[5] The eigenvalue for the resulting equation was .727, indicating considerable power in separating the opponents and supporters of McClory's motion. The canonical correlation (eta) was .649. On the McClory vote, a solid majority of both political parties opposed the motion. This suggests that the minority of supporters might be less swayed by norms of *go-along get-along* that often govern House voting behavior. Because the gun vote was the most lopsided of the issues considered in hypothesis five, we have included here a measure of bipartisanship, which indexes the degree to which a congressman typically votes with the majority when both parties support or oppose an issue jointly. We reason that this variable should enter the discriminant equation because the vast majority of congressmen are, as of the Ninety-fifty Congress, unwilling to move the gun control controversy away from a totally open politics, and thus those willing to do so might appear to be mavericks on numerous issues where a solid majority of both parties share a consensus. As the figures in Table 3 illustrate, this variable did enter the discriminant equation.

The discriminant equation reveals a vector in one-dimensional space, with the group centroid of the McClory opponents at .444 and with the group centroid of the McClory support at -1.630. Hence, the standardized discriminant coefficients in Table 3 indicate how much each variable pushes toward one group centroid or the other. A negative coefficient, for example, would move the representative closer to the McClory supporters. The coefficients in Table 3 indicate the relative weights of each variable in locating a representative along the discriminant vector. Using the classification function coefficients derived from this analysis, we correctly classified 83% of the vots on McClory's motion. As the results reveal, all but the lobbying hypothesis contribute to the equation, and all these variables enter in the predicted direction.

TABLE 3
Variables Discriminating Supporters and Opponents
of McClory's Motion

	standardized discriminant coefficients	statistical significance
ADA Rating	-.93773	.000
Bipartisanship	.41914	.000
% Urban	-.33327	.000
Size of Electoral Majority	-.28168	.000
% College Educated Among Constituents	-.17889	.008

CONCLUSION

Closed politics are antithetical to democratic processes, while open politics represents mass democracy in its most unencumbered form. In this age of bureaucracy and professionalism where, as Weber envisioned, experts exercise control through a reliance on specialized knowledge, a large number of social problems have been shifted from the arena of open politics into a more balanced or even closed politics. The dual forces of bureaucracy and democracy balance many social policies between the claims of expertise and the demands of common wisdom. Gun control is one of these policies. An intense minority with a cultural heritage derived from historical conditions now passed maintain an eternal vigil through their lobbies and stand ever ready to petition government whenever politicians consider the gun control issue. Only under conditions of unusual violence have these intense feelings given some ground to the temporary demands of an otherwise inattentive majority who favor gun regulation. NRA's electoral threat appears real to many congressmen, although its lobbying efforts through mass mailings more likely reinforce the will of congressional supporters than control the decisions of congressmen. In opposition, there are bureaucratic forces with some supporters in Congress that seek to move the gun control matter into a more balanced politics, where potential public hysteria is countered by the expertise of bureaucratic professionals. At this point in twentieth century American politics, the forces toward professional control are weaker than the forces toward open politics in the gun control controversy. Supported by a majority mobilized through tragedy and violence, it is likely that this matter one day will shift further into the bureaucratic arena, and the revised accommodation of expertise to common wisdom likely will weaken the forces demanding an open politics in the gun control controversy.

NOTES

1. Data derive from the *Congressional Quarterly*. Ratings based on the percentage of designated votes favoring the group's position on selected policy matters. All differences are significant beyond the .000 level.

2. It is obvious from the size of these averages that many representatives had little more than token opposition in the past general election. Much the same applies to primary elections. At the national level, competitive party elections never give the winning candidate more than 65% of the vote, so we used this figure to identify 184 congressional districts that appeared to have active party competition in the 1976 general elections. For these 184 districts, those opposing McClory's motion earned an average 56.6% of the vote, while those supporting McClory's motion earned an average of 55.3% of the vote. The difference between these two means is not statistically significant (.235) and, what is more important, the supporters of McClory's motion had a slightly smaller average electoral percentage than did those voting against McClory's motion. Such mixed results suggest a need for the multivariate analysis that follows later in this section.

3. The correlations between the latent dimension and each vote are: McClory's motion on ATF = .57, Assassination Committee Funding = .63, NSF Research Vote = -.71, Civil Rights for Inmates = -.71, Spouse Abuse Program = .67, Victim Compensation Program = .63, Civil Rights of Gays = -.75, and Legal Services for the Poor = .71. The one underlying dimension accounts for 52% of the total vector space. Negative signs on some of the correlations merely reflect what congressmen were voting for on that bill, amendment, or motion. In some instances, a positive vote opposed further fedral extensions. On the NSF vote, for example, the yea vote implied a reduction in the NSF budget for biological, behavioral, and social sciences research programs. If the votes are coded to represent support for federal involvement, then all signs would be positive.

4. F-level for entry required significance at the .01 level, and the tolerance level required that any new variable entering the equation have at least 50% of its variance left unexplained by the variables in the equation. Hence, there is no problem of multicollinearity, and the equation is significant at the .000 level.

5. For the discriminant function, we have data for a total of 386 congressional districts. To enter the equation, a variable had to be significant at the .01 level, and a strong tolerance requirement was set at .1.

D. Laureen Snider
Queen's University

6

REVISING THE COMBINES
INVESTIGATION ACT
A Study in Corporate Power

The Combines Investigation Act is the major federal act which seeks to regulate business activity throughout Canada. It is ostensibly an attempt by the state to intervene in the affairs of the business sector, to curb any excesses for the benefit of all citizens.

There are two predominant theoretical views on the nature, form, and intention of government regulations. Laws, of course, are a quintessential part of such regulations, but the term encompasses less formal social controls as well. The consensus/pluralist school (Rose, 1967; Parsons, 1937, 1951; Bell, 1960) argues that it is the role of the polity, those who are responsible for decision-making in the public sector (politicians and civil servants) in all levels of government, from the municipal to the federal, to carry out the wishes of the majority in the electorate, insofar as this is possible. Policies are formulated to reconcile diverse interests and prevent conflict. This often means interfering with the power and privileges of the rich and powerful to benefit the poor and powerless. No assumption is made that all the diverse groups are equally effective in making their voices heard, or that some groups are not more powerful or "strategic" than others, but pluralist/consensus theorists argue that any group, if they feel strongly enough about an issue, and if there are enough of them, *can* be effective; and that no one group dominates the political process in a fashion that is either permanent or overwhelming. Government regulations, to these theorists, are *rules formulated by politicians and civil servants which attempt to resolve or prevent conflicts by redressing the balance of power between different interests.*

The conflict/Marxist theorists see government regulation quite differently. Starting out from the premise that the state exists ultimately to defend and further the interests of the ruling class, they tend to see government regulation as a tool which serves to preserve the (very unequal) status quo. "The state" is comprised of those who occupy key decision-making posts in the political elite (prime ministers and cabinet ministers at the federal and provincial levels plus municipal officials with key territories or responsibilities, in the Canadian case); in the civil service (this includes commissioners in the important agencies); in the military; and in the judiciary (see Miliband, 1974: 50). Although in traditional Marxist theory, the state was seen as the "executive committee of the bourgeoisie," run by and for the ruling class, it is now argued by some that it operates more effectively when staffed by middle- and upwardly mobile working-class people. Government regulations that seem to benefit the underclasses, which aim to restrict the power or privileges of the ruling class, have their origins in social conflict, and specify as little reform as is necessary to pacify the spokesmen of whichever "cause" is at issue. They may even be promoted by ruling class members to get rid of small competitors by driving up costs in the regulated area (Kolko, 1962; Bliss, 1974). Government regulations for Marxist/conflict theorists are *rules formulated by the state which aim ultimately to maintain the power and privileges of the ruling class.*

THE COMBINES INVESTIGATION ACT:
DESCRIPTION

The key piece of Canadian legislation directed at large corporations is the Combines Investigation Act passed in 1889. Originally passed as a section of the Criminal Code of Canada, it dealt only with conspiracies to fix prices, suspected mergers, and suspected monopolies. The sanctions laid down were maximum fines of $4,000 or two-years imprisonment for individuals; or a maximum fine of $10,000 for corporations. In 1910 the "Combines Act" was passed, which set out maximum fines of up to $1,000 per day for individuals and corporations. (The prosecuting authorities, usually the Crown, used their discretion in deciding whether to lay charges under the Criminal Code or the act.) Over the years, maximum sanctions were increased (in absolute if not relative terms), the legislation was removed from the Criminal Code, and auxiliary offenses were added: price discrimination or predatory pricing in 1935; refusal to supply goods and resale price maintenance in 1952; and misleading advertising or misleading price representation in 1960. From 1960 until January 1, 1976, when the latest revisions went into effect, the act contained five main sections.[1] Section 32 made it illegal to conspire or arrange with another person to "limit unduly" the facilities to manufacture any article, or to "prevent, or lessen unduly" competition in the manufacture or production of any article, and to thereby increase the price. This was an indictable offense carrying a two-year prison sentence. Notice that the Canadian Act applied only to articles or commodities that "may be the subject of trade or commerce" and not to service industries such as professions, banks, or real estate. However, it was not illegal to exchange information relating to statistics, standards, credit, trade terms, research and development, as long as this exchange did not lessen competition unduly. Due to the inclusion of the word "unduly," none of these behaviors were prohibited outright.

Section 33 provided that everyone "who is a party-to-the formation of a merger or monopoly is guilty of an indictable offense and is liable to imprisonment for two years." Section 34 forbade certain trade practices, such as selling to one purchaser on different, more favorable terms than to competitors for goods like quality and quantity, or selling products at different prices in different areas of Canada, or at unreasonably low prices in order to eliminate or lessen competition. This was also an indictable offense with a maximum two-year prison sentence. Misrepresenting the price at which an article is ordinarily sold in order to promote its sale was an offense punishable on summary conviction. Section 37 prohibited publishing false, deceptive, or misleading advertisements on pain of a five-year prison term. Section 37 also prohibited as a summary offense the publication of performance or efficiency guarantees that were not based on a proper test (as defined by the government). Finally, section 38 prohibited resale price maintenance, the attempt by a wholesale dealer to set prices for retail merchants, as an indictable offense with a maximum two-year prison term. Refusal to supply goods was also prohibited here, but only if the seller "had reasonable cause to believe" that the retailer was using the goods as loss leaders in misleading advertising campaigns or not providing proper servicing. Thus, defenses were built into the law on resale price maintenance.

Investigations could be initiated by an application from six Canadian citizens, as direction from the minister of Consumer and Corporate Affairs, or by a member of the prime enforcing body, the Restrictive Trade Practices Commission (RTPC), through the Director of Investigation and Research. To initiate an inquiry, they could act whenever they believed an offense had been or was about to be committed. The investigation was carried out by the RTPC, composed of four government appointees, who could take evidence and make a report, but were unable to exercise any direct sanctions without applying to a judge. The reports were public unless the minister interfered "in the public interest," but the inquiries were always private.

HISTORY OF THE LEGISLATION

The Combines Act was passed in 1889 largely through the efforts of two grocers who had been excluded by their competitors from a gigantic scheme to fix the price of sugar. The Dominion Wholesale Grocers Guild had refused to supply sugar to any merchant who attempted to cut prices. Because sugar then accounted for 40% of the grocery trade, the two outraged retailers lobbied Parliament for antitrust legislation. The Conservative party, then in power, apparently went along with this in order to outflank their political opposition, and convened a committee which eventually led to passage of a bill ostensibly outlawing combines. However, because the legislation was worded so that a combine had to be engaged in *unlawfully* as well as *unduly* restricting trade, it was virtually unenforceable— only one prosecution was launched before 1900. Then, in a revision, the word "unlawfully" was dropped. Opinions are divided as to whether this was accidental (Stanbury, 1975) or purposeful, a real attempt to put teeth into the legislation (Gosse, 1962: 75). In any event, action was taken against five combines between 1900 and 1910. The targets were primarily American firms operating in Canada. (At this stage in the development of the Canadian economy, American interests did not have the strategic power and control that they have since gained over Canadian resources, and thus they were a popular and politically expedient target then.) It is ironic—and prophetic—that neither the investigations nor the legislation had the slightest effect on the wholesale grocers association whose combine had instigated the whole process. Old price-fixing arrangements stayed in effect; new ones in such commodities as rice, molasses, and starch, were negotiated in 1890 and 1891. As Bliss points out: "The only change . . . was that the press was no longer supplied with the details of decisions, although the trade press still had inside information" (Bliss, 1974: 34). Meanwhile, mergers were continuing apace. Between 1900 and 1910, seventy-two were recorded (Weldon, 1966: 233), mostly the result of the Canadian elite buying up smaller operations in order to reduce competition. There was still no mechanism by which the government automatically took responsibility for sniffing out and punishing illegal acts; the onus was put on six private citizens to swear out affidavits before a judge and apply for an investigation. It was quite obvious from the revisions of 1910 that Mac-Kenzie King, the U.C. Cabinet Minister then responsible for the act, and presumably the government on whose behalf he was acting, had no intention of hurting business or businessmen. He felt, underneath it all, that businessmen were not criminals and that any antisocial acts they committed could be controlled by the adverse publicity resulting from an inquiry under the act.

World War I led to the establishment of a permanent board of investigation and prosecution, but in 1919 its powers were declared to be in the field of civil law, and thus "ultra vires" under the division of powers granted to the federal government by the British North America Act, the Canadian Constitution. However, even before its demise, the board was not an unqualified success. A commissioner who resigned from it, pointed out that there was blatant interference from the government, especially the cabinet, who were terrified that the board would "tread on the toes of important business interests" (Goff, 1975: 43). The history of the ensuing amendments, in 1923, 1935, 1952, and 1960, shows how new behaviors were brought under the act, new sanctions proposed, and existing sanctions revised. At each stage, however, proposals were weakened or eliminated in the face of business opposition. As a result, by the mid-sixties it was obvious to all disinterested groups that the act was basically ineffective, and the Economic

Council of Canada was requested to undertake a critical review of competition policy which would serve as a basis for a complete overhaul of the existing legislation. An act designed to promote competition, and to replace the Combines Investigation Act, was drawn up shortly thereafter.

REVISIONS: 1969-1977

It is the history of these proposed, wide-ranging revisions that I wish to discuss. The weaknesses of the Combines Investigation Act as it stood in 1969 were well known to those interested in antitrust law and widely acknowledged. Specifically, fines for all offenses were too low, both in practice, often in the legislation; the wording of several crucial passages rendered larger sections of the act virtually unenforceable (for example, sections affecting mergers, monopolies, and resale price maintenance); many business abuses, such as bid-rigging, were not covered by the act, nor were any industries in the burgeoning service sector. As a result, enforcement was weak and spotty—in the twenty-two years between 1951 and 1972, only eighty-nine cases were brought to court under sections 32, 33, 34, and 38. Of these, ten were acquitted, and twenty-two were found guilty but were not fined; their sole "punishment" was an Order of Prohibition, a legal order directing the offenders to cease breaking the law. More significantly, under 10% of the formal inquiries initiated led to the pressing of charges. In many cases, this was because convictions could not be obtained, even though it was quite obvious an offense had been committed, due to the wording of the act. Fewer cases involving powerful dominant companies proceeded to the prosecution stage than did those involving small concerns (Snider, 1977: 170-182; Snider, 1978: 150-153). There had never been a court decision to reverse a merger or monopoly, and only one successful prosecution had been achieved in this history of the act. Even the trade practices section banning false advertising and misleading price representation, the most simple legislation from an enforcer's point of view, had seen only 346 cases prosecuted from its inclusion in the act in 1960 until 1973, and the most common fines assessed were $200 for large or dominant companies, and $100 for nondominant and unincorporated concerns (Snider, 1978: 155).

In response to these problems, certain changes to tighten up and improve Canada's laws in this area were recommended in the report of the Economic Council of Canada (Economic Council, 1969). On June 29, 1971, Bill C-256, the Competition Act, was given first reading in the House of Commons by Ron Basford, the Minister of Consumer and Corporate Affairs. The bill, based on the Economic Council's proposals, contained many provisions which were strongly proconsumer and procompetition. The legislation proposed a complete scrapping of the Combines Investigation Act—with its many amendments, built-in defenses, and poorly worded sections—and its replacement by an aptly titled Competition Act.

Some of the major changes that were proposed are detailed below:

(1) A specific list of trade practices and marketing techniques were banned outright. These included price-fixing, bid-rigging, limiting the production or distribution of supplies and service, preventing new competitors from entering the market, and refusing to supply certain merchants or wholesalers. Thus, the word "unduly," which had caused so many combines' cases to be dropped because convictions could not be secured, was finally to be eliminated.

(2) An independent tribunal, composed of three appointed members and entitled the Competitive Practices Tribunal, was to be set up to rule on mergers, some suspected monopolies, and other noncompetitive practices. Its powers were civil, not criminal; thus it could act with speed and dispatch, eliminating some of the problems inherent in prosecuting cases involving powerful defendants under criminal law. (Problems persisted despite the institution of "strict liability" for certain classes of offenses.)

(3) The act was extended to cover service industries as well as "items of trade and commerce."

(4) The four defenses which had been provided for those charged with resale price maintenance were eliminated.

(5) To determine whether advertising was misleading, the court were directed to employ the "credulous man" test rather than the "reasonable man" test. That is, if a rather naive and unsophisticated person would be deceived, the advertising could be declared misleading and subject to penalties.

REACTION: "APRES MOI, LE DELUGE"

Interestingly enough, the very early responses to the bill were not uniformly negative from the press or the business community. Several newspaper editorialists hailed it as a landmark of sorts, a significant advance for consumer interests. And an important business paper said:

> The Competition Act, in name and intent, is—positive. It introduces new economic criteria in place of deadly and unworkable legal sanctions [Financial Times, July 5, 1971: 8].

Academics were found criticizing the bill for not being strong enough in places (though those in professional faculties disliked the ban on professional fee setting).

However, this initial reaction was not to last. A big business took a good look at what the new legislation actually proposed, the forces of opposition were set in motion, and soon overwhelmed both the media and the government. In response to the legislation, 197 briefs were submitted in the following two-year period. Only two of these were from organizations promoting the consumer interest; and only four in all (the two consumer submissions plus two from academics) were uniformly favorable to Bill C-256. Of the total 161 briefs were from business or trade firms or organizations, and a further ten represented corporate interests in different disguises. The combined financial resources opposing the legislation were staggering. As the business response became better known, through increasing public relations efforts, the media response, especially that of the most respected Canadian newspapers, became more and more hostile, until it was hard to find an editorialist or financial writer who would defend the legislation. Lobbying continued behind the scenes too, with members of the cabinet, key civil service employees, and run-of-the-mill members of Parliament and senators becoming persuaded of the terrible nature of Bill C-256.

The business community objected to both specific features of the bill, and to its philosophy and intent. The two provisions that came under the most attack were the institution of the Competitive Practices Tribunal, and the outright prohibition of certain anticompetitive practices. The Tribunal, it was argued, was too powerful, too unaccountable to anyone for its decisions, and too arbitrary. Businessmen would never know what was legal and what was not, and the climate of uncertainty would be bad, not just for business, it was claimed, but for the whole country. The exact opposite objection was raised to the list of prohibited activities. These, it was claimed, were too concrete and inflexible. Combines and similar activities should only be illegal under certain circumstances, which the courts would determine. (Why *this* uncertainty was acceptable while that created by the Competitive Practices Tribunal was not, was a question which was never raised, much less dealt with.) Specifically, the corporate sector wanted the provision "unduly" put back into the legislation, especially in the sections referring to illegal combines.

However, the intense campaign against the bill was not limited to specific proposals. The objections advanced in the media, and in the corridors and lobbies of Parliament, also singled out the bill as an attack on the entire "free enterprise" system.[2] Freedom of contract would be stifled, business growth would be halted, business confidence would be eroded, and investment would falter and halt.[3] Creativity would be restricted, especially in advertising, and jobs would be lost. Emotional, "ad hominem" attacks also appeared. The will was written by "ivory tower" academics and/or bureaucrats hopelessly out of touch with the "real world," people who had "never had to meet a payroll." Such people were obviously incapable of understanding the needs and interests of the business elite.

The voice of the small entrepreneur, who stood to gain by the legislation (if enforced as written), was effectively lost in the stampede of big business interests, as was the voice of the independent university professor of business or economics or law. So, of course, was the voice of the consumer.

The financial power of those opposing the legislation was impressive—one lobbying group which presented a brief represented thirteen firms with combined revenues of 7.8 billion dollars. Such corporate concerns had arrays of lawyers prepared to argue all sides of competition policy in every public and private arena. Consumer groups and academics usually delivered their briefs in person or had a lawyer do it, in a one-shot effort. The business lobby, in contrast, was continuous, invisible, and intense, shifting from cabinet ministers to senior civil servants to back bench members of Parliament. It undoubtedly operated to great effect on the private level, because we know that high-level politicians and top corporate executives are closely interrelated through common club memberships and marriage ties (Clement, 1975).

GOVERNMENT RESPONSES

It did not take long for those in government to respond.[4] A first step was to change personnel. The minister of Consumer and Corporate Affairs, responsible for the Competition Act, was transferred to a different portfolio to January 1972, six months after the bill was introduced. This was just the beginning. Between 1972 and 1977, there were to be *seven* different ministers. The senior civil servants in the department were similarly replaced and transferred out—there were three different deputy-ministers in this same time period, and the director and deputy-directors of the Committee for Investigation Act were both replaced. (They were not, as far as we can tell, fired or demoted; they were merely rendered impotent.) As a result, virtually all of the top-level elected and appointed officials who had worked on Bill C-256, most of whom were committed to the new competition policy, had been removed by the end of 1973. The continuing personnel changes after that date had the effect of ensuring that none of the new people in the jobs long enough to really grasp the salient issues or to become effective spokesmen for a view opposing the powerful business interests.

A more obvious concession came on July 18, 1973, when the then-Minister of Consumer and Corporate Affairs, Herb Gray, announced that changes in competition policy were going to be made in two stages. Thus, Bill C-256 was scuttled. In its place, instead of a new act, there were to be a series of amendments to the old Combines Investigation Act, with the sections on combines and misleading advertising to be introduced first. The structurally crucial areas of monopoly and merger policy were to be delayed.[5]

Nor were these the only victories for business interests. When the Stage I amendments were finally passed by the House and the Senate (they took effect on January 1, 1976), the legislation looked very different from what had been proposed for each substantive area in 1971. Most of these changes represented a concession to the big business lobby.

A key one was the reinsertion of the word "unduly" with reference to combines. Prosecutors will still be unable to get convictions unless they can show that a conspiracy restricted trade unduly. Thus, the number of cases successfully prosecuted will continue to be small, and the majority of inquiries will lead to no action.

Second, the Competitive Practices Tribunal was eliminated from the Stage I amendments. Thus, only by attaining a successful conviction in a court of law (a lengthy, expensive, and often unsuccessful process), can combines be stopped; no civil remedies are now possible. The individual or firm wronged by a restraint of trade still has the right to sue, of course. In fact, to encourage litigants, a provision for awarding them double damages was suggested in the origin bill. (Sections of the parallel American legislation allow for treble damages.) However, this too was roundly attacked, and in the final version, civil litigants can receive only the damages they can prove they suffered, plus court costs.

With regard to misleading advertising and price representation, the credulous man test was dropped, and the reasonable man test reinstituted. Pyramid and referral sales schemes were only prohibited under certain conditions, not in an outright fashion. The defense of "due diligence" was restored, meaning that corporations are not liable for a misleading advertising offense if they can prove they exercised a reasonable amount of supervision and care over their subordinates. The provisions relating to bid-rigging were weakened so that convictions would be harder to obtain.

Finally, in relation to section 38, resale price maintenance, the four defenses which were eliminated in the original version of the Competition Act were all restored in the amended one, ensuring that convictions remain very hard to secure. Effective control over resale price maintenance, which is especially crucial to the survival of small retailers and to the ability of consumers to buy products at discounts, is still to be achieved in the Canadian marketplace.

SUMMARY AND CONCLUSIONS

The preceding description does not exhaust discussion of all the ways in which the corporate lobbyists influenced the policy process. It is obvious to even a casual observer that the state has been pretty effectively outmuscled in this confrontation with the corporate elite. The consensus/pluralist view that laws function to curb the excesses of certain (powerful) groups in the interests of the majority does not seem to be borne out by the history of revisions to the Combines Investigation Act.

The results lead one, instead, to a conflict/Marxist interpretation. It is too simplistic to argue that the corporate elite dominate policymaking because of their overwhelming financial resources. This is an important, but not conclusive, factor. Some unions, plus organizations such as the American or Canadian Medical Associations, have spent just as much money on lobbying their respective legislatures, and have emerged far less successful. No, the reasons for the success of the corporate section lie elsewhere, and are related, I would argue, to their direct and indirect control over resources in the liberal democratic state. The direct power comes from their control over the life chances of most Canadians through their near-monopolization of employment opportunities, and their dominance over the health of the economic system. Their indirect power is ideological. The views and interests of the corporate elite are predominant forces which shape, to varying degrees, the world view of everyone else in the society. The versions of reality which coincide with their views are termed "legitimate" and "responsible," while versions that reflect the interests of opposing groups are deemed irresponsible at best, dangerous or treasonous at worst (Miliband, 1974; Marchak, 1975). This does not mean that laws do not change, or that reforms are never instituted. Some reforms *were* retained in the latest revisions to the Combines Investigation Act—service industries are now covered, for example, and the number of illegal trade practices has been extended. However, such reforms will be resisted as long as possible by the corporate elite, and instituted only when they are seen as necessary to stave off greater threats to the status quo, of which they are the main beneficiaries. As Turk has said:

Those who are most advantaged by a legal system have historically been extremely unlikely to permit the system itself to be destroyed, or even radically altered by—relatively bloodless methods. . . . Indeed, it is difficult to imagine a set of conditions that would persuade the historically successful political-economic elites to give up their classic strategy of resisting democratic pressures as long as possible [Turk, 1974: 21].

NOTES

1. All quotes in this section are taken from, and refer to, the *Combines Investigation Act*, Office Consolidation. (Ottawa: Information Canada, 1972).

2. In classic theory, competition, of course, was the very bulwark of the free enterprise system.

3. The extent to which these changes are potentially true is a measure of the extreme structural dependence of the capitalist economic system on a small number of people, the corporate elite. Because the state has very little control over whether or where the profits (which are seen as private property) will be disposed of, key corporate decision-makers can make their own prophecies come true, simply by taking their money out of the country or putting millions in Swiss banks. "Loss of confidence" is the bogeyman of the liberal democratic state. As Miliband has said:

> The point is—that the control of business of large and crucially important areas of economic life makes it extremely *difficult* for governments to impose on policies to which it is firmly imposed.—Business, in the very nature of a capitalist system of economic organization is immeasurably better placed than any other interest to (lobby) effectively, and to cause governments to pay much greater attention to its wishes and susceptibilities than to anybody else [Miliband, 1974: 132-133, emphasis in original].

4. The federal election in 1972 was probably one more factor in the governing party's about-face. It is thought that the decreased ideological levels, was a major factor in their near-defeat in the 1962 elections. The lesson was apparently not lost on them, as the lack of top-level support for even amended versions become more and more obvious. When the much-revised bill was introduced in Parliament in 1973, there was not one other cabinet minister present in the House of Commons.

5. They were introduced in Parliament on March 16, 1977, and have been stalled ever since. As this is written (February 28, 1979), in preparation for a spring election, the present minister of Consumer and Corporate Affairs is promising to scrap the last bill, and introduce yet another one in the next week. In view of the history of the legislation, this latest bill may well be introduced with great fanfare and publicity, and die unnoticed and unpassed on the order paper at the end of the present parliamentary session.

Linda S. Anderson
Mankato State University

7

THE DETERRENT EFFECT OF CRIMINAL SANCTIONS
Reviewing the Evidence

If one listens to legislators or public officials it becomes obvious that there is a firm belief that "punishment deters crime," and more particularly, that more severe penalties will deter most effectively. Deterrence theory is in evidence at the core of our legislation and throughout our judicial proceedings. The adherence to deterrence as a "truth" plays a major role in the legal ideology of common law systems of criminal law. It is, therefore, critically important to a sociology of criminal law in such countries that the theory's validity be assessed. Sociologists, criminologists, economists, and political scientists have devoted considerable effort trying to resolve the underlying empirical questions. On the surface the classical writings of Bentham (1948) and Beccaria (1963) may appear to provide clear-cut models for establishing such evidence, but in actuality, neither Beccaria nor Bentham expressed his ideas about punishment and its consequences in the form of a theory with testable propositions. Gibbs (1975: 5) notes that the ideas of the classical theorists were close to systematic theory, and that they can be reduced to one generalization: "The rate for a particular type of crime varies inversely with the celerity, certainty, and severity of punishments of that type of crime." He believes, however, that deterrence research has not proceeded far enough beyond that broad generalization.

Empirical tests are confounded by the definition of deterrence as the *omission* or curtailment of behavior because of the perceived risk or fear of punishment for the behavior. It is thus an *"inherently unobservable* phenomenon" which is testable only via inference (Gibbs, 1975: 3). It becomes crucial that social scientists know what it is they are studying and what evidence is needed to confirm or disconfirm its existence. Gibbs introduces additional reasons for the inherent difficulties in testing deterrence empirically. He explains that there are ten "preventive consequences of punishment" of which deterrence is only one. The other nine preventive mechanisms[1] may reduce criminal behavior for reasons totally unrelated to perceived risk or fear of punishment.

Despite the confusion as to interpretation, and the imprecision in the specification of the theory and the associated testable propositions, a large body of deterrence research has accumulated. The remainder of this essay will address the question of whether there is any cohesive support for the belief that punishment deters crime.

CAPITAL PUNISHMENT LITERATURE

The question about the deterrent effects of punishment was at one point considered settled by many sociologists. This followed a number of examinations of the death penalty and its deterrent impact on homicide (e.g., Schuessler, 1952; Savitz, 1958; Sellin, 1967) which found no patterns indicative of deterrence. The consistency of the findings led to the premature conclusion by some that the deterrence issue was resolved. Eventually, however, this "resolution" was challenged, due to methodological defects of these studies, and the realization that even if those findings *were* definitive about the negligible deterrent effect of capital punishment, this would not be sufficient reason to generalize to other types of punishment or other offenses. Further support for reopening the debate about capital punishment has come from recent research, much of it by economists. Ehrlich (1975a) claimed that his lagged regression analysis demonstrated a pure deterrent effect of capital punishment. Others, however, have criticized Ehrlich's work, and the issue is still being actively debated (see, e.g., Bowers and Pierce, 1975; Passell and Taylor, 1977; Passell, 1975; Ehrlich, 1975b, 1977).

ECOLOGICAL STUDIES

Aside from the brief period of time following the initial capital punishment studies, the deterrence issue has never been considered resolved either favorably or unfavorably. The late 1960s saw an increasing amount of attention being paid to addressing the question. Beginning with Gibbs (1968) and Tittle (1969), a number of studies began to appear which used official crime statistics and compared the aggregate data on crime rates for different geographical units. In most cases the studies examined objective measures of the severity and certainty of punishment for specific noncapital offenses. On the whole the studies found inverse relationshipos between crime rates and the certainty of punishment. Some inverse relationshps were found for severity of punishment as well, although such support was less consistent than that for the certainty of sanction. None of the studies seemed to address the issue of celerity of punishment, despite its central position in classical deterrence theory. In an early review of much of the pertinent evidence, Tittle and Logan (1973) concluded that the studies had basically been supportive of deterrence.

This interpretation of the findings has been questioned, based on claims that there are serious problems inherent in the use of aggregate data to examine the deterrence question. Andenaes (1975), for example, notes that the research has not made an effort to separate the deterrent effect of imprisonment from its incapacitative effect. While he does cite evidence that the incapacitative effect may be minimal, Andenaes, like Gibbs (1975), recognizes that we may be attributing to deterrence an effect on crime rate due to another preventive mechanism. (See Blumstein et al., 1978, for further discussions of incapacitation and deterrence.)

Similarly, while efforts have been made to consider alternative explanations for the inverse relationship between sanctions and crime by examining possibilities such as system capacity or overload models (e.g., Geerken and Gove, 1977; Pontell, 1978) those studies have also been inconclusive. Even if we are able to eliminate such alternatives, the possibility of competing preventive effects means that findings based solely on relationships between crime rates and sanctions can at best be interpreted as addressing the preventive effects of punishment as a whole.

Another difficulty with these studies is found in the operationalization of the major variables: certainty and severity of punishment. While a wide range of sanctions is applied for the index crimes typically studied, imprisonment has been the determinant of certainty and severity for many of the studies to the exclusion of fines, jail sentences, or probation. For a number of offenses such as auto theft, the probability of a prison sentence may be quite low, while the probability of some other sanction may be much greater. For such offenses, measures of the certainty of imprisonment and measures of severity based on time in prison would not equal the actual certainty and severity of *punishment*. Such difficulties make it hard to accurately assess the deterrent effect of either certainty or severity. Just as the capital punishment literature does not enable us to draw conclusions regarding deterrence in general, the interpretation of the comparative studies using aggregate data must be limited to the effects of *imprisonment* on crime rates (Andenaes, 1975).

An additional problem inherent in any ecological approach to the study of deterrence is that the distinction between general and specific deterrence has been blurred, because the crime rates are used without regard to the prior records of the offenders involved. While the crime rate for first offenders might be indicative of general deterrence, the rates for recidivists refer to specific deterrence, and the combination of the two categories of offenders precludes an interpretation of findings with regard to general deterrence (Cousineau, 1973).

It has been repeatedly noted (e.g., Andenaes, 1975; Chiricos and Waldo, 1970; Gibbs, 1975; Henshel and Carey, 1975) that the major difficulty with this past research concerns the use of actual sanctions rather than those perceived by the general public. If individuals are unaware of the actual certainty and severity of sanctions, then those sanction characteristics are not likely to act as constraining forces on behavior. If people *are* deterred, this is a function of their perceptions of legal consequences, rather than a function of the objective certainty or severity of sanctions. Past studies using aggregate data have assumed that public perceptions of punishment properties are accurate. Research evidence such as that done by the Assembly Committee on Criminal Procedure in California (1975), however, suggests widespread public ignorance on such issues.

Erickson and Gibbs (1978) addressed this issue by examining both objective and perceptual measures of sanctions, and their relationship to crime rates (officially measured). They noted that an interpretation of Bentham and Beccaria's ideas leads to the basic premise that objective certainty of punishment is directly related to perceived certainty of punishment, which in turn is inversely related to the crime rate for the population under consideration. It thus becomes crucial to show not only that perceived sanctions and crime rate are inversely related, but also that the relationship between objective certainty and crime rate occurs *through* the perceived certainty of punishment. Their findings did reveal negative relationships for the crime rate with both objective and perceived certainty of arrest, but there was no evidence that the link between objective certainty and crime rate was perceived certainty. (Instead of approaching zero, $r_{oc.p} = -.54$.) Such a finding casts serious doubts on the existing evidence regarding general deterrence. While it may be argued that objective certainty operates on the crime rate through other preventive mechanisms as well as through perceived certainty, Erickson and Gibbs (1978) note that that argument cannot be made if negative relationships between objective certainty and crime rate are taken to be evidence of deterrence.

The preceding comments have emphasized the difficulties inherent in interpreting much of the existing deterrence literature. There has been little closure on any of the relevent issues; as Tittle (1978: 32) has noted, "one cannot presently demonstrate a pure deterrent effect using ecological data, but neither can it be ruled out." Many researchers have felt the need to address deterrence questions by using alternative methodological approaches.

PERCEPTUAL SURVEY RESEARCH

As previously noted, the deterrence doctrine is based on psychological premises, and therefore perceptual variables must be central to any empirical tests. In fact, Erickson and Jensen (1977: 305) believe that the doctrine can be reduced to a single assertion: "That when a criminal act is contemplated the *perception* of a high risk of a swift and severe reaction by legal officials is a sufficient condition for omitting that act." Recently the number of investigations accepting such a premise has increased dramatically, although the techniques for testing deterrence via perceived sanctions have been almost as numerous as the number of investigations. Table 1 summarizes several characteristics of twenty-one recent studies which used perceptual data to address issues of general deterrence. These studies all included information on perceived sanctions and their relationship to criminal and/or delinquent behavior, although this was by no means the only concern of the studies, or even a primary concern in several cases. The table is included here to help illustrate some of the reasons why the deterrence question remains unanswered despite considerable amounts of research and attention.

All of the studies used either a questionnaire or interview format to survey groups of nonformally sanctioned individuals. The studies differed as to the number of criminal or delinquent behaviors individually examined (zero to fifteen) while seven of them utilized indexes combining several behaviors. While most of the studies relied on self-reported measures, two of them used official data for behavior meas-

TABLE 1
Summary Characteristics of Studies Using Perceptual Data
To Examine General Deterrence

	Jensen	Waldo & Chiricos	Burkett & Jensen	Bailey & Lott	Grasmick & Milligan	Kraut	Silberman
1. Year	1969	1972	1975	1976	1976	1976	1976
2. Respondents of Study	males, grades 7-12	under-graduates	high school seniors	sociology students	adult drivers	under-graduates	under-graduates
3. # Respondents	1,588	321	1,056	266	187	606	174
4. Location of Study	CA	FL	WA	Mid-west	Mid-west city	PA	PA
5. Instrument[a]	Q	I	Q	Q	I	Q	O
6. Behavior Measure[b]	SR & O	SR	SR	SR	SR	SR	SR
7. # Behaviors Examined	O	2	1	5	1	1	9
8. Use of Behavior Index	+[c]	-	-	-	-	-	+
9. Self-Referred Certainty	-	+	+	+	-	+	+
10. Other-Referred Certainty	+[e]	+	-	-	+	+	-
11. Self-Referred Severity	-	-	-	+	-	+	+
12. Other-Referred Severity	-	+	-	-	-	-	-
13. Celerity	-	-	-	-	-	-	-
14. Unit of Analysis[h]	I	I	I	I	I	I	I
15. Longitudinal Design	-	-	-	-	-	-	-

Rows 9–13 are grouped under the vertical label "Type of Perceived Sanctions."

ures, and one utilized an estimation of future deviance. Although this is not indicated in the table, those using self-report measures of behavior had varying time periods for which the behavior was reported, and coding of behavioral responses ranged from uncategorized frequencies to several different categorizations.

TABLE 1 (Continued)

	Teevan	Teevan	Anderson	Chiricos et al.	Erickson et al.	Grasmick & Appleton	Longshore	Meier & Johnson	Minor
1.	1976a	1976b	1977	1977	1977	1977	1977	1977	1977
2.	high school students	sociology students	freshmen in college	high school students	high school students	adult drivers	sociology students	adults ages 18+	adults
3.	421	191	300	426	1,700	166	142	632	274
4.	Ontario Canada	Canada	FL	FL	AZ	Midwest City	CA	IL	FL
5.	Q	Q	I	Q	Q	I	Q	Q & I	I
6.	SR	SR	SR	SR	SR	SR	SR	SR	SR
7.	2	2	4	0	15	1	10	1	5
8.	-	-	+	+	-	-	+	-	+
9.	+[d]	-	+	-	-	-	-	-	+
10.	+	+	+	+[f]	+	+	+	+	-
11.	+[d]	-	+	+[f]	-	-	-	-	-
12.	+	+	-	-	-	-	+	+	-
13.	-	-	+	+	-	-	-	-	-
14.	I	I	I	I	A	I	I	I	I
15.	-	-	+	+	-	-	-	-	-

The perceived sanction measures with which the behaviors were correlated varied in both operationalization and categorization. In all but two cases the sanction measures were offense-specific. The perceived certainty and severity measures for all but one case referred to the time of the survey, the exception being Teevan's (1976a) measures of certainty and severity which involved recall of prior perceptions. Some investigators examined both perceived certainty and perceived severity of punishment, while others chose to focus on certainty alone. A few examined perceived celerity of punishment as well. Measures

TABLE 1 (Continued)

	Peck	Teevan	Thomas	Tittle	Erickson & Gibbs
1.	1977	1977	1977	1977	1978
2.	high school stu-	13-20 year olds	stu- dents grades 8-12	per- sons ages 15+	adults
3.	571	396	2,249	1,993	1,200
4.	Pacific North- west	Ontario Canada	VA	NJ, IA & OR	AZ
5.	Q	Q & I	Q	I	I
6.	SR	SR	SR	FD	O
7.	1	6	0	9	10
8.	-	-	+	-	-
9.	+	-	-	+	-
10.	-	+	+[g]	-	+
11.	-	-	-	-	-
12.	-	+	+[g]	-	-
13.	+	-	+[g]	-	-
14.	I	I	I	I	A
15.	-	-	+	-	-

a. Q indicates a questionnaire administration; I indicates an interview.
b. SR indicates self-report measures; O indicates official data; FD indicates self-esti- mated future deviance.
c. + indicates that a specific characteristic was used or found in the particular study referenced; — indicates the characteristic's absence or nonuse.
d. Measure of recall of prior perceptions.
e. General rather than offense-specific measure.
f. General measure averaged across offense-specific responses.
g. Items are part of a scale combining other-referred certainty, severity, and celerity items, and are not analyzed separately.
h. I indicates that individuals are used as the unit of analysis; A indicates that acts are used as the unit of analysis.

which were both "other-referred" and "self-referred" were employed by those examining certainty and severity. The former category includes the possibility that some general- ized other(s) would be sanctioned for proscribed behavior, while the latter includes cases where the respondent or someone like the respondent would be sanctioned for the behavior.[2] No one study used all of the possible types of sanction, and the variation between studies brings the comparability of findings into question. If it is the case that perceived sanctions differ when an individual speculates about the risks for himself versus the risks for the generalized other, as has been suggested (e.g., Claster, 1967; Teevan, 1975; Waldo and Chiricos, 1972), then the studies may actually be examining different variables.

The unit of analysis also varied among the different studies. Most of them examined the relationship between perceived sanctions and criminal behavior among individuals, but Erickson and his colleagues (Erickson and Gibbs, 1978; Erickson and Jensen, 1977) examined the relationship between crime rates and perceived sanctions with types of acts as the unit of analysis. This technique seems to be subject to some of the criticism levelled at the earlier ecological studies. By utilizing sanction measures consisting of average perceived certainty, and by using categorical rates or measures or central tendency for frequency of behavior, they have modified the psychological level of analysis deemed so necessary for deterrence studies. It is conceivable that combining individual perceptions and behaviors into groups of measures masks any distinct individual differences (even those as basic as sex differences). Such a methodology also precludes a longitudinal analysis which could examine individual changes in perceived sanctions and behavior over time.

Although it was not possible to indicate this in the table, the studies also differed in the degree of support for deterrence which was found. Though little consistent support was generated for either perceived severity or perceived celerity, almost all of the findings for perceived certainty were in the hypothesized negative direction. The strength of support varied, however, not only from study to study for the same offense, but from one offense to another within specific studies. For example, Waldo and Chiricos (1972) found strong support for deterrence for the offense of marijuana use (gamma = –.84 using self-referred certainty), yet Bailey and Lott's (1976) study found only very weak support for the same relationship (r = –.09). Further, the Waldo and Chiricos (1972) study found only moderate support for the offense of petty theft (gamma = –.31). In addition, cross-study comparisons are made difficult by the use of different measures of association, e.g., gamma and Pearson's r. (See Anderson, 1977, for a discussion of this issue.) In general, the studies provide some support (of undetermined strength) for the idea that perceived sanctions and criminal behavior are inversely related, but this support varies with different types of sanction and behavior measures, and for different offenses. Recalling Gibbs' (1975) pessimistic comment that separate deterrence models might be necessary for every distinct offense, Grasmick and Appleton (1977) have suggested the development of offense typologies as a more parsimonious approach for future deterrence work. Until such a time, however, there is little of a cohesive nature which can be said to summarize findings of perceptual studies such as those presented in Table 1.

Furthermore, even the highly general statement that perceived certainty and criminal behavior are inversely related for most of those studies must be qualified. An interpretive problem arises when controls for extralegal conditions are introduced. For example, Erickson and Jensen (1977) found that perceived certainty and behavior measures were inversely related, as hypothesized by deterrence theory. When perceived seriousness of offense was partialled out, however, the relationship disappeared, due to the high degree of collinearity between perceived certainty and the seriousness measure. The authors suggested that an individual's perception of a given offense as "serious" is a function of that individual's perception of the certainty of punishment for committing it. Seriousness was seen by Erickson and his colleagues as an indication of social (extralegal) condemnation of crime; if punishment serves to generate and/or maintain this social condemnation, its function is normative validation (Gibbs, 1975), rather than deterrence.

Because aggregate level research did not control for social condemnation, past researchers may have incorrectly drawn conclusions about deterrent effects. This same criticism may be levelled at much of the perceptual research which has also neglected to control for preventive mechanisms such as normative validation, but at least perceptual research can more easily be modified to accommodate these controls. Furthermore, for the perceptually based studies, not all of Gibb's rival causal mechanisms are actually possible as competing explanations. Because four of them (incapacitation, punitive surveillance, reformation, and normative insulation) are relevant only once punishment has been applied, studies dealing with the threat of punishment rather than its actual imposition need not be concerned with them. Clearly, studies should continue to consider competing mechanisms as has been done by Silberman (1976) with moral commitment, by Longshore (1977) with adherence to legal norms and stigmatization, by Grasmick and Appleton (1977) with stigmatization, and by Minor (1977) with belief in legal norms.

LONGITUDINAL STUDIES

A serious problem with past perceptual deterrence studies has been the ambiguous time-ordering of variables. The deterrence doctrine clearly addresses the effects of sanctions on *subsequent* behavior. Yet, many of the studies utilized measures of behavior which *preceded* the measurement of perceived sanctions, based on an assumption of perceptual stability (Anderson, 1977; Silberman, 1976). The common "backwards" ordering confounds the interpretation of empirical findings, both because a logical case can be made that behavior may itself have an effect on perceived sanctions, and because the assumption of perceptual stability underlying such ordering may not exist. Anderson (1977) examined the latter possibility, and found that perceptual stability did not clearly obtain from one year to the next with a college student sample. She also examined the viability of "experiential" effects of behavior on perceived sanctions, and suggested that most of the existing perceptual studies have actually examined those effects, rather than deterrent effects.

In recognition of this causal ambiguity, many researchers (e.g., Burkett and Jensen, 1975; Teevan, 1975, 1976a; Kraut, 1976; Silberman, 1976) have suggested the need for longitudinal designs in order to ensure that sanction measures precede behavioral measures of behavior. Several researchers have already completed longitudinal studies which address deterrence issues (Anderson, 1977; Biron, 1977; Biron and Cusson, 1979; Chiricos et al., 1977; Thomas, 1977). In lieu of a panel design, Teevan (1976a) and Tittle (1977) both attempted to address meaningfully the causal order problem. Teevan's study correlated behavior with respondents' recollections of prior perceptual states, while Tittle measured current perceptions of certainty of punishment for marijuana use and respondents' perceived likelihood of their own *future* marijuana use. Neither method had dealt adequately with the problem of causal order, because each necessitated the substitution of a new and untested assumption in place of the previous assumption of perceptual stability. Teevan had to assume that current recollections of prior perceptual states are accurate and unaffected by intervening behavior, while Tittle had to assume the accuracy of behavioral predictions.

While perhaps well-suited to addressing the causal order difficulties, panel studies may be accompanied by other difficulties. First of all, attrition from one data collection stage to the next can cause interpretational problems. Another difficulty may stem from the nonanonymity required in order to recontact respondents for subsequent data collection stages. For general deterrence studies, another serious difficulty with the longitudinal design is that if the period of time between measurement of sanctions and measurement of subsequent behavior is short, very little criminal behavior will be reported by a generally law-abiding population. The time lag cannot be made too long, however, or recall becomes a problem. In addition, the longer the time lag, the more likely are other intervening variables besides the previously measured perceived sanctions to affect the behavior. Such problems were indentified in several of the longitudinal studies conducted thus far (Anderson, 1977; Chiricos et al., 1977).

Longitudinal studies also have the capability to examine changes in perceived sanctions over time, and to correlate those changes with behavior changes. Such an analysis would seem to directly address some of the unresolved deterrence issues. Unfortunately, there is no easy way to separate the ongoing influences of behavior and perceived sanctions on each other during periods between data collection waves. If the relationship between sanctions and behavior is processual and ongoing, even a longitudinal approach will not eliminate the causal ambiguity of deterrence research.

CONCLUSION

It has not been possible to address more than a few aspects of the deterrence model here, and even these aspects have been dealt with in a cursory fashion. Attention has been focused on studies of general deterrence to the exclusion of work on specific deterrence. Studies involving experiments and retrospective research were excluded as were comments about the often recognized need for deterrence research to focus on the interaction between certainty and severity. Nor have we addressed recent suggestions that deterrence be integrated with social control theory (Meier and Johnson, 1977; Minor, 1977).

It should be apparent from the areas which were addressed—particularly the perceptual survey research—that there is not yet any clear or cohesive support for deterrence. At this point it remains an unverified criminological "truth." Based on the difficulties of testing deterrence, it may very well remain unverified. The most reasonable path toward resolution would seem to involve establishing consensus on smaller areas, perhaps by focusing on particular categories of offense. It is not likely that we will ever be able to generalize to the whole deterrence issue without qualification. Ironically, although we may feel a need to narrow the focus to specific types of offenses, we may simultaneously come to the conclusion that we must broaden the underlying questions being examined. We may wish to determine the overall effects of punishment on behavior, because of the difficulties inherent in trying to distinguish deterrent effects from the other possible effects of punishment. As we proceed with the examination of the effects of sanctions on behavior, we may continue to assert that punishment *does* deter crime; if we do so, however, we need to establish when, how, and under what conditions it does so.

NOTES

1. The other mechanisms are incapacitation, punitive surveillance, enculturation, reformation, normative validation, retribution, stigmatization, normative insulation, and habituation (Gibbs, 1975: 57-93).

2. The alternative use of other terms for these categories, such as "general certainty" and "personal certainty" (Teevan, 1975) may erroneously imply that the self-referred measure is not a general deterrence measure. In fact, *both* types of measure examine general deterrence, as long as those responding have not experienced legal punishment.

Richard A. Ball
West Virginia University

A THEORY OF PUNISHMENT
Restricted Reprobation and the
Reparation of Social Reality

The problem of punishment is one of the most serious facing contemporary criminology. A decade ago, Hart (1968) suggested that while interest in this topic of punishment has never been greater, public discussion has never been more confused, largely because of modern skepticism about the dogmas of utilitarianism and retributionism. While once it appeared that these older notions would give way to the newer doctrine of reformation, this goal too has come under increasing fire (Allen, 1959; Martinson, 1972), turning some to resurrection of the earlier approaches (Morris, 1974; van den Haag, 1975; von Hirsch, 1976; Wilson, 1974). Now we are more confused than ever before. Some have come to despair of reason in the search for answers, urging that we must do whatever "works." It turns out, however, that reasonable people disagree over the definition of "effectiveness" and that some reject a surrender to expediency even when the expedient can be defined.

In what follows I will urge a new perspective on punishment, one which rests on the concept of "restricted reprobation." This perspective treats punishment as one basis for the systematic negotiation of collective social reality and for the enlightened reparation of that reality, which is a necessary condition of social life. Its advantages become

135

clear in light of the strengths and weaknesses inherent in the older doctrines of retribution, utility, and reformation.

RETRIBUTION

The doctrine of retribution is usually couched in the language of moralism, a language which has serious limitations. The essence of the idea is both positive and negative; it involves a theme of reciprocal rights and duties. On the positive side, there is the right, even the duty, to punish infractions. On the negative side, there is the restriction that only the guilty may be punished. The doctrine of retribution is usually accompanied by the ideas that the function of punishment is the "negation" or annulment of evil, that the punishment must be "fitting" to the crime, and that offenders have a "right" to punishment and ought to be treated as moral ends rather than as instrumental means (Quinton, 1954: 513). The justifications may be subdivided into a number of categories, among them being retaliation and expiation.

The problems of retribution as a justification for punishment have been recognized for centuries. The retaliation theme is rooted in the idea of vengeance, but to revenge there is no end. The expiation theme can be equally pernicious, for who is to speak in the name of the alleged deity who demands the atonement? Cohen (1940), who is an advocate of the retributive position, has admitted that there are additional questions to which he can find no answer. "For the state to exercise the same amount of fraud or brutality on the criminal that the criminal exercised on his victim would be demoralizing to any community" (Cohen, 1940: 1010). And how can society determine the exact amount of suffering experienced by the victim? How is it possible to measure the severity of a punishment when different offenders may suffer differently the same official sanction? Is the same fine equal punishment if levied on a poor offender as well as a rich one? Is a specific prison sentence really identical punishment if passed on one individual with close family ties and another with more friends inside than outside?

In spite of these criticisms, however, the doctrine of retribution was slowly gaining strength behind the scenes even before the recent spurt of interest. Nearly forty years ago, Cohen (1940) presented his cogent argument to the effect that the human tendency toward retribution should be accepted and institutionalized rather than uselessly resisted. More recently Henry Hart (1958) has suggested a return to consideration of the moral aspect of crime, and Hall (1960) has stressed the concept of moral responsibility as the most important factor to be considered in a theory of punishment.

This developing interest in the doctrine of retribution seems to represent at bottom a reaction to the relatively amoral position assumed by the utilitarians and the advocates of reformation. These latter perspectives were alleged to be more "rational" and "scientific," and hence more "humanitarian." But it is just these assertions which have troubled the new retributivists. Lewis (1953), for example, strikes a firmly moral note in his insistence that the so-called "humanitarian" theories are really *immoral* because they deny the concept of "desert."

> My contention is that this doctrine, merciful though it appears, really means that each one of us, from the moment he breaks the law, is deprived of the rights of a human being.
>
> The reason is this. The humanitarian theory removes from Punishment the concept of Desert. But the concept of desert is the only connecting link between punishment and justice. It is only as deserved or undeserved that a sentence can be just or unjust. I do not here contend that the question, Is it deserved? is the only one we can reasonably ask about a punishment. We may properly ask whether it is likely to deter others and to reform the criminal. But neither of the last two questions is a question about justice [Lewis, 1953: 225].

I believe that Lewis has perceived something that is easily overlooked. There are two sides to the doctrine of retribution. While one side demands punishment, the other restricts it. Thus, the retributivists insist on punishment, but they are unanimous in rejecting lynch law, which would seem the most speedy and certain means of exacting revenge. To throw out the entire doctrine as an outmoded moralism is to ignore the advance which it represented, the legitimation of punishment through the concept of justice. There is an important kernel of theoretical value in the position of the retributivists, as there is in the doctrines of utility and reformation. The problem is that each of these is caught in the coils of certain older assumptions. Retributivists might benefit from a broader view of morality. Different formulations are possible, perhaps even a synthesis which can incorporate most of the insights they have given us, but in a different person.

UTILITY

The utilitarian approach was an attempt to supplant moralistic notions through the use of purely rational methods. Punishment could no longer be justified on the "barbarous" grounds of vengeful retaliation, nor were the "superstitious" theories of expiation to be entertained by reasonable men. In keeping with the new ideas of the rising middle class, the justification for punishment was found in its practical usefulness. The new language was that of rationalism, and it left little room for moral concerns. The aim was expediency; the dominant themes were incapacitation and deterrence.

The utilitarian doctrine has not delivered what it promised. Aside from the question of its amorality, the basic flaw seems to be an overly rationalized conception of humanity. There is little evidence to the effect that the criminal proceeds in the extremely calculative manner ascribed to him by the utilitarians. Since Bentham wrote, we have learned much from Freud, from Gestalt psychology, from the sociology of knowledge, and from a variety of other sensitive sources, and we have seen a century of alienation, anxiety, and atrocity on a grand scale. What is more, it has become clear that the utilitarian position operates at a level of logical abstraction which ignores vast human differences—"What will deter one man will have no effect upon another, yet will crush a third. Their method is based on the theory that all men are mentally alike and something like themselves" (Coddington, 1946: 166).

Even if this model of humanity were accurate, there is another very serious problem. Stripped to its essentials, the theme of incapacitation is a purely negative notion which accomplishes little in the long run and may actually aggravate the problem. As for the deterrence theme, it is frankly based on the presumed power of fear. But can any society hope to produce long-term obedience by fear? And if methods can ever be devised, what will be the price of their application? Before one responds with a plea for the primacy of logic over morality, he ought to consider where the logic leads. To be logically consistent, for example, society would have to punish most heavily those offenses which there is great temptation to commit but which are at the same time so minor that offenders will not be constrained by any feelings of guilt (Hawkins, 1944: 206).

Actually, if we examine the doctrine of utility closely we find that it does not deal with punishment at all. To understand this is to attain a clearer understanding of both the doctrine of utility and the nature of punishment. The utilitarian position deals not with punishment as much as with the assignment of *penalties*. As opposed to punishments, which always carry a social stigma, penalties are purely quantitative sanctions, often merely "price-tags" put on offenses (Feinberg, 1965: 397). If one can afford to pay the penalty for a particular offense (e.g., a parking ticket), he may simply commit it in a situation where he might otherwise be inconvenienced.

Yet, in spite of all its problems, the utilitarian approach contains valuable theoretical insights. It represents a break with the traditionalism of the doctrine of retribution and provides part of the foundation for a critique of complacent moralism. To see the law simply as a rational means for the incapacitation of the offender and the deterrence of further offenses was to tear away centuries of mysticism. This made possible more rational codification of law and led to more logical consideration of the entire enterprise. Just as the limitations of the doctrine of retribution can be traced to an excessively narrow moralism, the central deficiency of the utilitarian perspective lies in an excessively narrow rationalism. Any theory which seeks a more adequate foundation must incorporate the instrumental rationalism of the utilitarians into a broader vision of human life.

REFORMATION

The doctrine of reformation, as it lost much of its early moral tone through the impact of utilitarianism, took on the language of sicnece. There are two principal problems with this doctrine, and they are closely related. The mitigative theme was a humanitarian attempt to reduce the unnecessary harshness that accompanied punishment. It tended to place restrictions on cruelty, but basic punishment was left untouched, neither justified nor eliminated. As for the corrective theme, it stressed the aim of reform but concentrated on a search for the most effective methods, essentially within the taken-for-granted context.

Much of the problem with the doctrine of reformation lies in its apparent amorality. This is a less serious problem with the merely mitigative approach than it is with the corrective approach. As Lewis (1953) has reminded us, the technical "expert" tends to operate without the idea of justice, which is a moral and not a scientific concept.

Martinson (1972), among others, has cited evidence that the "Dangerous myth" of treatment actually operates so as to allow alleged experts to hold the criminal for much longer periods of time than are permitted under community conceptions of justice, aggravating the original problems of social adjustment.

Yet, what has been said of the doctrines of retribution and utility must also be said of the reformation approach. Despite its defects, it has made possible an advancement in perspective, suggesting that situations can be improved, that we can accomplish more than a return to whatever context prevailed prior to the crime. Perhaps, however, the issue is not so much the reformation of the offender as it is the restoration of an acceptable relationship between the offender and his society, something that may require adaptation on *both* sides. Along with the positive insights of the doctrines of retribution and utility, such a perspective leads us toward a broader theory of punishment, one which stresses restricted reprobation in the interests of the reparation of collective social reality.

RESTRICTED REPROBATION AND REALITY REPARATION

Given the inadequacies of the three traditional theories of punishment, it is time to take a closer look at an approach which might be capable of incorporating the insights of each without their respective limitations. This approach may be grounded on a more general theoretical position in which social life is treated as a socially constructed reality, which is developed, sustained, and altered by the continued interaction of the members of a given society. According to the reality constructionist position, which is drawn in turn from the tradition of the sociology of knowledge, social institutions begin in recurrent patterns of interaction which becomes typifications of mutually understood categories of action. In this way social situations are defined, and shared meaning is established. A symbolic universe is constructed; everything is put in its "right" place. Society makes sense to its members. The essential point is that no matter how solid the social order appears, the sense of mutual reality is always precarious. "The constant possibiltiy of anomic terror is actualized whenever the legitimations that obscure the precariousness are threatened or collapse" (Berger and Luckman, 1967: 103). Society is thus faced with two fundamental problems. The first problem is how to sustain the collective definitions of reality which allow common interpretations and shared expectations. The second problem is how to provide sufficient flexibility so that social reality can be continually constructed and reconstructed as conditions change. This two-sided process involves the *reparation of social reality*.

The basic functions of punishment are *symbolic*, as Feinberg (1965: 399) says: "Punishment is a conventional device for the expression of attitudes of resentment and indignation, and of judgements of disapproval and reprobation, either on the part of the punishing authority himself or of these 'In whose name' the punishment is inflicted." He locates the distinction between punishments and mere penalties in the fact of a difference in expressive function. "Punishment, in short, has a *symbolic significance* largely missing from other kinds of penalties (Feinberg, 1965: 399, emphasis in original). In contrasting criminal law and civil law, Henry Hart (1958: II, A, 4) has noted that, "What distinguishes a criminal from a civil sanction and all that distinguishes it, it is ventured, is the judgement of community condemnation which accompanies its imposition." A somewhat similar view is expressed by Andenaes (1968).

Unfortunately, these theorists have been unable to achieve a consistent and theoretically grounded position, leading some to conclude that these insights represent nothing more than the old retributivist position in disguise (Walker, 1967). There is some truth in this suspicion, but only because the older doctrines retain such latent influence. Clarification of the new approach depends upon a systematic examination of the most critical issue facing social theory—the relation of the individual to society.

The Perspective of Society

From the perspective of society punishment serves to affirm the *norm of reciprocity* (Gouldner, 1960). Although it is not necessary to revert to social contract theory here, it seems reasonable to expect that those who conform to the taken-for-granted requirements of group life will tend to feel resentment toward those who gain an illegal advantage through the violation of the social expectations. Reciprocity is expected: the social bond rests to a considerable extent on this reciprocity. If it is not forthcoming the others involved in the web of social interaction feel cheated. "It is only reasonable that those who voluntarily comply with the rules be given assurance that they will not be assuming burdens which others are unprepared to assume" (Morris, 1968: 477). This is a major part of an important political reality that should not be overlooked by these who wish to reform the law and still retain its public support. The fact is that the public demands punishment (Walker, 1967), and that there is a certain justice to the demand (Hawkins, 1944). Undoubtedly, there is an unnecessarily heavy weight of "moral indignation" consisting of repressed hostility toward the offender, especially among those who may lack the courage to commit the offenses they secretly find so attractive, but this is reason to *restrict* social reprobation, not reason to abolish it.

By drawing a symbolic line, formalized reprobation also provides *an absolution of those who did not participate in the offense* (Feinberg, 1965: 408). More generally, to punish the offender alone is to affirm the boundary which has been constructed between that which is crime and that which is not crime. Struggles over law are struggles over the collective definition of reality. In any such contest, the outcome may be more a matter of social power than social justice. Among other things, this means that the machinery of legal definition must be made public, and that arbitrary power must be restricted in the name of justice.

From the perspective of the society another punishment also serves for the *restraint of the individual*. The history of humanity is the history of the emergence of the individual from the constraints of the larger group. This has made more and more likely a clash of interests. Now to operate solely in the interests of society as these are perceived by these influential over the legal apparatus is to risk social stagnation. The relatively free individual may be the best asset of a society faced with rapid social change, for societies with such individuals are endowed with a greater flexibility. If this is true, it would imply that severe restrictions should be placed on the extent to which society is allowed to restrain individuality. But surely homicide, rape, assault, environmental pollution, price fixing, and marketing of unsafe products cannot be permitted under current conceptions of justice.

Hawkins (1944: 209) moved toward a clarification of the moral argument here in his statement that the "Genuine sense" of retribution "is not a crude tit for tat but a restraint put upon human activity which has been corrupted by being devoted to evil," tracing this point of view to Aquinas, who maintained that equity requires that a human being be deprived of the good against which he acts because his act implies some degree of rejection. According to this view, punishment consists essentially of a loss of a portion of self-determination.

Anyone attempting to consider the functions of punishment "from the point of view of society" must, of course, be very careful not to reify the social system. If this happens law becomes just another justification for the *status quo* when it may also be an instrument for social change. Restricted reprobation may also be employed so as to "repair" the collective social reality in the sense of advancing conceptions of social justice.

The Perspective of the Individual

It is equally important to social theory that punishment be examined from the point of view of the individual, but here too we must avoid the dangers of reification. This is often forgotten. Reification of the individual is reflected in the writings of many existentialists, who tend to emphasize the image of a completely free individual in an apolitical situation (Gerber and McAnany, 1967: 502). In much of the work of Sartre, for example, morality and law are treated as mere techniques by which the bourgeoise maintains its hegemony over social reality. What he does instead is to reify the lone individual into a sort of superman, a totally free and independent force who must struggle against the social psychological tyranny of the social system. This is a fictional individual existing outside social reality.

Describing the process of self-regulation by which societies maintain themselves, Nadel (1953) has pointed out that individuals conform for two different reasons: (1) an inclination to do so and (2) a perception of a favorable balance of premiums and penalties. Utilitarianism has done an admirable job of arguing the latter point, but the emphasis there has led to neglect of the whole issue of shared values on which basic inclinations rest. *If there is no utility for me in obedience to a particular law, why should I expect to obey it?* Out of fear alone? The answer seems to be that the system of social cooperation must be valued in itself. I will support those laws which are advantageous to me, but I will also support at least some of those which are not, simply because I value the whole enterprise. Here the symbolic and expressive aspect of the law should not be underestimated, particularly in modern, industrial societies which tend to lack powerful symbols of social identification which help to sustain the individual.

But can we reasonably expect reprobation to have any effect at all on someone who has repudiated the law? The answer here must begin with a denial of the premise. The data do not support this stereotype of the offender. Instead, the evidence suggests that most *offenders are fairly conventional* about nearly everything, and that they are able to violate the law because of a variety of excuses and not a rejection of society. The effect of reprobation will vary with the extent of commitment to social norms and with self-image. In the case of amateur shoplifters the effect seems to be very powerful. In the case of hardened professional criminals it may be negligible. And in any case, it is worth emphasizing that the level of reprobation of which we are speaking can be varied and that mere loss of self-determination is a real punishment in an individualistic society.

It is also possible for an individual to believe in a law and yet violate it in circumstances of *extreme temptation.* Commitment to the norms may not have been strong enough to prevent the offense, but it may still be strong enough to force the offender to recognize the justice of the punishment (McTaggart, 1896: 486). If the impact of the punishment coincides with the recognition of its justice, punishment may even make possible a more vivid appreciation of the rights of others. That is a condition difficult to achieve, but it loses no value as a social goal.

The punitive character of the criminal law may also work to the social advantage of the offender in circumstances in which the individual accepts a certain principle, perhaps even urges it on others, yet *fails to see rather obvious applications* when these run counter to his own narrow interests. McTaggart (1896) has cited as examples those who believed murder to be sinful but, nevertheless, fought the most unfair duels, as well as those who professed to believe in the right of all to liberty but continued to hold slaves. As he says, "For it is only possible to accept the general law, and reject the particular application, by ignoring the unanswerable question, "Why did not you in this particular case practice what you preach?'' (McTaggart, 1896: 486). It is possible, he adds, to ignore a question, but it is more difficult to ignore a tangible punishment supported by the community.

Following McTaggart, one may find other instances in which punishment can have a positive effect on the offender. One example is the situation in which social authority is accepted; the problem being that the offender *did not know* that the act was outlawed. The official reprobation calls the illegality to his attention in no uncertain terms. Again, however, there is a clear distinction to be made between the perspective of restricted reprobation and the older doctrines of punishment. This becomes clear when we examine the consensual prohibition on the application of ex post facto legislation. Why should such a prohibition exist? If punishment is a matter of retribution the offended certainly have a right to revenge whether the offense was or was not legally prohibited at the time of its commission, and expiation will still allow for atonement. The doctrine of utility, of course, allows punishment simply to incapacitate the offender or to prevent future offenses. Finally, the reformation approach would certainly insist that the offender is in need of rehabilitation even if society had been lax in seeing to it that his particular pathological behavior was outlawed sooner. Our theory suggests that the prohibition of retrospective legislation exists for two related reasons. The idea of *restricted* reprobation calls attention to the point that society is a collection of individuals each of whom is entitled to be treated, in Kantian terms, as an end and not a means. The individual is to be protected against the awesome power of society which must state the consensual reality in advance. Second, the concept of *reprobation* rather than retribution, utility, or reformation emphasizes that society is also a symbolic union and not a mere artifact of power or rational planning or self-righteous expertise.

In all of this there is no need to contribute to the degradation of the individual as each of the older doctrines of punishment has been accused of doing. There has been a basic confusion of degradation with disgrace (McTaggart, 1896: 492). To force an awareness of offenses, such as the injury of others who have done no harm, is not necessarily to degrade an individual. It must be remembered that "the effort to make life more decent always involves a struggle against opposing forces," and that "we must hate evil if we really love the good" (Cohen, 1940: 1017). This is to say that our definition of social reality must be consistent. It is the *act* which society must denounce, and it is not necessary to degrade the offender to denounce the act. Here the quality of the reprobation is crucial.

What about the Kantian doctrine which holds that a human should never be treated as a means but an end? Does a theory of restricted reprobation as the expression of reality reparation conflict with this precept? The answer is that what Kant actually said was that we should never treat humanity *only* as a means, but always *also* as an end. As Rashdall (1924: 303) has pointed out, to punish a human being in the interests of society is to treat the person as a means, but the right to be treated as an end is not thereby violated as long as his good is treated as of equal importance with that of other human beings. Much of the problem here can be traced to the arbitrary distinction between individual and collectivity. From this point of view what goes to society must come from the individual, and vice versa. But that is hardly the case. Both benefit from a consistent, just definition of social reality which can be collectively altered with the passage of time.

CONCLUSION

Let us consider the conditions for effective punishment, given our theory. In addition to the reasonable utilitarian principles of *certainty* and *celerity*, we must add certain principles derived from the more moralistic doctrine of retribution, particularly those revolving around the principle of *desert*, which demands that the guilty, but only those, be punished and that the punishment "fit" the crime. These principles must be reconsidered in terms of the thrust of the doctrine of reformation, the principle of *change*, applied to both the individual and to society.

In terms of our theory it is especially important that the state maintain its symbolic effectiveness by upholding the collective values. If the representatives of the state are themselves corrupt, the state loses this symbolic authority which it only holds in trust. This is not true under the older doctrines. The "right" to retribution is not diminished by one's own guilt, for it is merely a formalized revenge. The right to deter the potential offender is not lost simply because one is equally guilty, for successful deterrence would at least hold down the totality of criminal activity. And the right to treat the offender is certainly not lost simply because the physician turns out to be as ill as the patient. A properly grounded theory of restricted reprobation in the service of the reparation of collective social reality will hold the state as accountable as it holds the individual.

REFERENCES

AKERS, R. L. (1968) "Problems in the sociology of deviance: social definitions and behavior." Social Forces 46 (June): 455-465.

—— and R. HAWKINS (1975) Law and Control in Society. Englewood Cliffs, NJ: Prentice-Hall.

ALLEN, F. (1959) "Criminal justice, legal values and the rehabilitative ideal." Journal of Criminal Law, Criminology and Police Science 50: 226-232.

ALEXANDER, T. (1976) "It's time for new approaches to pollution control." Fortune (November): 128-131, 230-234.

ANDENAES, J. (1968) "Does punishment deter crime?" Criminal Law Quarterly 11: 76-93.

—— (1971) "The moral or educative influence of criminal law." Journal of Social Issues 24(2): 17-31.

—— (1975) "General prevention revisited: research and policy implications." Journal of Criminal Law and Criminology 66: 338-365.

ANDERSEN, G. E., R. FRIEDLAND, and E. O. WRIGHT (1976) "Modes of class struggle and the capitalist state." Kapitalistate (Summer): 186-220.

ANDERSON, L. S. (1977) "A longitudinal study of the deterrence model." Ph.D. dissertation, Florida State University.

Assembly Committee on Criminal Procedure [State of California] (1975) "Public knowledge of criminal penalties," pp. 74-90 in R. L. Henshel and R. A. Silverman (eds.) Perception in Criminology. New York: Columbia University Press.

AUERBACH, C. A. (1966) "Legal tasks for the sociologist." Law and Society Review: 1: 91-104.

AUGUSTINE (1952) The City of God. Chicago: Encyclopedia Britannica, Great Books of the Western World.

AUSTIN, J. (1954) The Province of Jurisprudence Determined and The Uses of the Study of Jurisprudence. New York: Noonday Press. (originally published in 1861)

BAILEY, W. C. and R. P. LOTT (1976) "Crime, punishment and personality: an examination of the deterrence question." Journal of Criminal Law and Criminology 67: 99-109.

BANKSTON, W. B. and J. B. CRAMER (1974) "Toward a macro-sociological interpretation of general deterrence." Criminology 12(3): 251-280.

BARNET, R. (1971) "The twilight of the nation-state: a crisis of legitimacy," pp. 221-242 in R. P. Wolff (ed.) The Rule of Law. New York: Simon and Schuster.

BARRETT, W. (1958) Irrational Man: A Study in Existential Philsophy. Garden City, NY: Doubleday.

BECCARIA, C. (1963) On Crimes and Punishments (H. Paolucci, trans.). Indianapolis: Bobbs-Merrill.

BECQUAI, A. (1977) "White collar plea bargaining." Trial magazine (July): 38-41.

BELL, D. (1960) The End of Ideology. Glencoe, IL: Free Press.

BENTHAM, J. (1948) A Fragment on Government and An Introduction to the Principles of Morals and Legislation (W. Harrison, ed.). New York: Macmillan.

—— (1970) An Introduction to the Principles of Morals and Legislation. Darien, CT: Hafner.

BERGER, P. and T. LUCKMANN (1966) The Social Construction of Reality. A Treatise in the Sociology of Knowledge. Garden City, NY: Doubleday.

BERK, R. A., H. BRACKMAN, and S. LESSER (1977) A Measure of Justice: An Empirical Study of Changes in the California Penal Code, 1955-1971. New York: Academic.

BIRON, L. (1977) "Norms, risk and status offenses." Presented at the annual meeting of the Society for the Study of Social Problems.

——— and M. CUSSON (1979) "La contrainte sociale et la délinquance." Groupe de Recherche sur l'Inadaptation Juvénile, Universite de Montréal. (unpublished report)

BLACK, D. (1972) "The boundaries of legal sociology." Yale Law Journal 81: 1086-1100.

——— (1976) The Behavior of Law. New York: Academic.

BLISS, M. (1974) A Living Profit: Studies in the Social History of Canadian Business, 1883-1911, Toronto: McClelland and Stewart.

BLUMSTEIN, A., J. COHEN, and D. NAGIN [eds.] (1978) Deterrence and Incapacitation: Estimating the Effects of Criminal Sanctions in Crime Rates. Washington, DC: National Academy of Sciences.

BOHANNAN, P. (1968) "Law and legal institutions." International Encyclopedia of the Social Sciences 9: 73-78.

BOWERS, W. J. and G. L. PIERCE (1975) "The illusion of deterrence in Isaac Ehrlich's research on capital punishment." Yale Law Journal 85: 187-208.

BOYDELL, C. L. and I. CONNIDIS (1974) "The administration of criminal justice: continuity versus conflict," pp. 290-311 in C. L. Boydell, P. C. Whitehead, and C. F. Grindstaff (eds.) The Administration of Criminal Justice in Canada. Toronto: Holt, Rinehart & Winston.

BURKETT, S. R. and E. L. JENSEN (1975) "Conventional ties, peer influence, and the fear of apprehension: a study of adolescent marijuana use." Sociological Quarterly 16: 522-533.

BURLING, R. (1970) Man's Many Voices: Language in its Cultural Context. New York: Holt, Rinehart & Winston.

CHAMBLISS, W. J. (1974) "Functional and conflict theories of crime," pp 1-23 in Module 17. New York: MSS Modular.

——— and M. MANKOFF (1976) Whose Law? What Order? A Conflict Approach to Criminology. New York: John Wiley.

——— and R. B. SEIDMAN (1971) Law, Order, and Power. Reading, MA: Addison-Wesley.

CHIRICOS, T. G. and G. P. WALDO (1970) "Punishment and crime: an examination of some empirical evidence." Social Problems 18: 280-289.

——— (1976) "Socioeconomic status and sentencing: an empirical assessment of a conflict proposition." American Sociological Review 40: 753-772.

——— L. S. ANDERSON, W. D. BALES, R. P. KERN, and R. PATERNOSTER (1977) Deterrence of Delinquency. Final Report to U.S. Department of Justice, LEAA. Gainesville: Florida State University.

CHKHIKVADZE, V. M. [ed.] (1969) The Soviet State and Law. Moscow: Progress.

CLASTER, D. S. (1967) "Comparison of risk perception between delinquents and non-delinquents." Journal of Criminal Law, Criminology and Police Science. 58: 80-86.

CLEMENT, W. (1975) The Canadian Corporate Elite. Toronto: McClelland and Stewart.

CLINARD, M. B. and P. C. YEAGER (1978) "Corporate crime: issues in research." Criminology 16 (August): 255-272.

CODDINGTON, F.J.O. (1940) "Problems of punishment." Proceedings of the Aristotlean Society 46: 155-178.

COHEN, M. R. (1940) "Moral aspects of the criminal law." Yale Law Journal 46: 1009-1026.

COLLINS, R. (1975) Conflict Sociology: Toward an Explanatory Science. New York: Academic.

Council on Environmental Quality (1970) Environmental Quality: The First Annual Report of the Council on Environmental Quality. Washington, DC: Government Printing Office.

——— (1976) Environmental Quality: The Seventh Annual Report of the Council on Environmental Quality. Washington, DC: Government Printing Office.

COUSINEAU, D. F. (1973) "A critique of the ecological approach to the study of deterrence." Social Science Quarterly 54: 152-158.

CRESSEY, D. R. (1978) "Criminological theory, social science, and the repression of crime." Criminology 16, (2): 171-191.

DAVID, R. and J.E.C. BRIERLY (1968) Major Legal Systems in the World Today: An Introduction to the Comparative Study of Law. London: Free Press.

DAVIES, J. C. III and B. S. DAVIES (1975) The Politics of Pollution. Indianapolis: Pegasus.

DESSION, G. (1955) "The technique of public order: evolving concepts of criminal law." Buffalo Law Review 5: 22-47.

DURKHEIM, E. (1933) The Division of Labor in Society (George Simpson, trans.). New York: Free Press.

——— (1973) "Two laws of penal evolution." (T. A. Jones and A. T. Scull, trans.). Economy and Society 2: 285-307.

DWORKIN, R. (1977) Taking Rights Seriously. Cambridge, MA: Harvard University Press.

Economic Council of Canada (1969) Interim Report on Competition Policy, July. Ottawa: Queen's Printer.

EDELHERTZ, H. (1970) The Nature, Impact and Prosecution of White Collar Crime. Washington, DC: Government Printing Office.

EDELMAN, M. (1964) The Symbolic Use of Politics. Urbana: University of Illinois Press.

EHRLICH, I. (1975a) "The deterrent effect of capital punishment: a question of life and death." American Economic Review 65: 397-417.

——— (1975b) "Deterrence: evidence and inference." Yale Law Journal 85: 209-227.

——— (1977) "The deterrent effect of capital punishment: reply." The American Economic Review 67: 452-458.

ENLOE, C. H. (1975) The Politics of Pollution in Comparative Perspective. New York: David McKay.

Environmental Protection Agency (1977) "EPA enforcement: a progress report." Washington, D.C.

——— (1978) "Recent developments in federal water pollution enforcement."

Presented at ALI-ABA Course of Study: Environmental Law, Washington, D.C., February 9-11.

ERICKSON, M. L. and G. F. JENSEN (1977) "The deterrence doctrine and the perceived certainty of legal punishments." American Sociological Review 42: 305-317.

——— and J. P. GIBBS (1978) "Objective and perceptual properties of legal punishment and the deterrence doctrine." Social Problems 25: 253-264.

——— and G. F. JENSEN (1977) "The deterrence doctrine and the perceived certainty of legal punishments." American Sociological Review 42: 305-317.

ERSKINE, H. (1972) "The polls: pollution and its costs." Public Opinion Quarterly 26, 1: 120-135.

EVAN, W. M. (1962) "Law as an instrument of social change." Estudies de Sociologia 2(August): 167-176.

FALLOWS, J. M. (1971) The Water Lords. New York: Grossman.

FAUST, F. L. and P. J. BRANTINGHAM (1979) Juvenile Justice Philosophy. St. Paul, MN: West.

FEELEY, M. M. (1976) "The concept of laws in social science: a critique and notes on an expanded view." Law and Society Review 10 (Summer): 497-523.

FEINBERG, J. (1965) "The expressive function of punishment." The Monist 49: 397-403.

FELLMETH, R. (1970) The Interstate Commerce Omission. New York: Grossman.

FRIEDMAN, M. (1962) Capitalism and Freedom. Chicago: University of Chicago Press.

FRIEDMANN, W. (1967) Legal Theory. New York: Columbia University Press.

FULLER, L. (1964) The Morality of Law. New Haven, CT: Yale University Press.

GEERKEN, M. and W. R. GOVE (1977) "Deterrence, overload and incapacitation: an empirical evaluation." Social Forces 56: 424-427.

General Accounting Office (1978) Handgun Control: Effectiveness and Costs. A Report to the Comptroller General of the United States. Washington, DC: General Accounting Office.

GERBER, R. J. and P. D. McANANY (1967) "Punishment: current survey of philosophy and law." St. Louis University Law Journal 11: 502-535.

GIBBS, J. P. (1968) "Crime, punishment and deterrence." Southwestern Social Science Quarterly 48: 515-530.

——— (1968) "Definitions of law and empirical questions." Law and Society Review 2(May): 429-446.

——— (1975) Crime, Punishment and Deterrence. New York: Elsevier.

GLENN, M. K. (1973) "The crime of 'pollution': the role of federal water pollution criminal sanctions." American Criminal Law Review 11, 4 (Summer): 835-882.

GOFF, C. (1975) Corporate Crime in Canada. M. A. Thesis, University of Calgary.

——— and C. REASONS (1978) Corporate Crime in Canada, Scarborough, Ontario: Prentice-Hall.

GOSSE, R. (1962) The Law on Competition in Canada, Toronto: Carswell.

GOULDNER, A. (1960) "The norm of reciprocity: a preliminary statement." American Sociological Review 25: 161-172.

GRASMICK, H. G. and L. APPLETON (1977) "Legal punishment and social stigma: a comparison of two deterrence models." Social Science Quarterly 58: 15-28.

——— and H. MILLIGAN, Jr. (1976) "Deterrence theory approach to socioeconomic/demographic correlates of crime." Social Science Quarterly 57: 608-617.

GREEN, M. J. (1972) The Closed Enterprise System. New York: Grossman.

GUNNINGHAM, N. (1974) Pollution, Social Interest and the Law. London: Martin Robertson.

GUSFIELD, J. P. (1968) "On legislating morals: the symbolic process of designating deviance." California Law Review 56: 54-73.

HABERMAS, J. (1975) Legitimation Crisis. Boston: Beacon.

HALL, J. (1960) General Principles of Criminal Law. New York: Basic Books.

HAMILTON, W. (1932) "Judicial process." Encyclopaedia of the Social Sciences 8: 450-456.

HART, H. (1958) "The aims of the criminal law." Law and Contemporary Problems 23: 401-420.

HART, H.L.A. (1961) The Concept of Law. Oxford: Clarendon.

——— (1968) Punishment and Responsibility. Oxford: Clarendon.

HAWKINS, D.J.B. (1944) "Punishment and moral responsibility." Modern Law Review 7: 205-208.

HENSHEL, R. L. and S. H. CAREY (1975) "Deviance, deterrence, and knowledge of sanctions," pp. 54-73 in R. L. Henshel and R. A. Silverman (eds.) Perception in Criminology. New York: Columbia University Press.

HOEBEL, E. A. (1954) The Law of Primitive Man. Cambridge, MA: Harvard University.

HOFSTADTER, R. (1963) Anti-Intellectualism in American Life. New York: Vintage.

——— (1967) The Paranoid Style in American Politics. New York: Vintage.

HYMES, D. (1961) "The functions of speech: an evolutionary approach," pp. 55-83 in F. C. Gruber (ed.) Anthropology and Education. Philadelphia: University of Pennsylvania Press.

In re GAULT (1967) 387 U.S. 1, 87 S. Ct. 1428, 18 L. Ed. 2nd 527.

JEFFREY, W. (1978) "The behavior of law: a view from the trenches." Chitty's Law Journal 26 (December).

JENSEN, G. F. (1969) "'Crime doesn't pay': correlates of a shared misunderstanding." Social Problems 17: 189-201.

KELLY, B. (1977) "Allied Chemical kept that kepone flowing." Business and Society Review 21(Spring): 17-22.

KENNETT, L, and J. ANDERSON (1975) The Gun in America. Westport, CT: Greenwood Press.

KITTRIE, N. N. (1971) The Right to Be Different: Deviance and Enforced Therapy. Baltimore, MD: Johns Hopkins Press.

KOLKO, G. (1962) Wealth and Power in America: An Analysis of Social Class and Income Distribution. New York: Praeger.

KRAUT, R. E. (1976) "Deterrent and definitional influences on shoplifting." Social Problems 23: 358-368.

KUHN, A. (1961) "Toward a uniform language of information and knowledge." Synthese 13(June): 127-153.

LANZA-KADUCE, L. (1978) "Distingegration or rebellion: the law-morality debate." M.A. thesis, University of Iowa.

LEMERT, E. M. (1970) Social Action and Legal Change: Revolution within the Juvenile Court. Chicago: Aldine.

LENSKI, G. (1966) Power and Privilege: A Theory of Social Stratification. New York: McGraw-Hill.

—— (1978) Human Societies: An Introduction to Macrosociology. New York: McGraw-Hill.

LeVINE, R. A. and D. T. CAMPBELL (1972) Ethnocentrism: Theories of Conflict, Ethnic Attitudes and Group Behavior. New York: Wiley.

LEVI-STRAUSS, C. (1966) The Savage Mind. Chicago: University of Chicago Press.

LEWIS, C. S. (1953) "The humanitarian theory of punishment." 20th Century 3: 5-12.

LLEWELLYN, K. (1930) The Bramble Bush. Some Lectures on Law and its Study. New York: Privately printed.

—— (1960) The Common Law Tradition: Deciding Appeals. Boston: Little, Brown.

—— (1962) Jurisprudence: Realism in Theory and Practice. Chicago: University of Chicago Press.

LONGSHORE, D. (1977) "Deterring crime: the effects of perceived sanctions and adherence to legal norms." Los Angeles: University of California. (unpublished)

LUKES, S. (1972) Emile Durkheim: His Life and Work. New York: Harper & Row.

MANNHEIM, H. (1965) Comparative Criminology (2 vols.). London: Routledge and Kegan Paul.

MARCHAK, P. (1975) Ideological Perspectives on Canada. Toronto: McGraw-Hill Ryerson.

MARTINSON, R. (1972) "The paradox of prison reform." New Republic 20: 19-28.

McTAGGERT, J. E. (1896) "Hegel's theory of punishment." International Journal of Ethics 6: 482-499.

MEIER, R. F. and W. T. JOHNSON (1977) "Deterrence as social control: the legal and extralegal production of conformity." American Sociological Review 42: 292-304.

MICHAEL, J. and M. J. ADLER (1933) Crime, Law and Social Science. New York: Harcourt Brace Jovanovich.

MILIBAND, R. (1974) The State in Capitalist Society. London: Quartet.

MINOR, W. W. (1977) "A deterrence-control theory of crime," pp. 117-137 in R. F. Meier (ed.) Theory in Criminology: Contemporary Views. Beverly Hills: Sage.

MORRIS, H. (1968) "Persons and punishment." The Monist 52: 476-479.

MORRIS, N. (1974) The Future of Imprisonment. Chicago: University of Chicago Press.

NADEL, S. F. (1953) "Social control and self regulation." Social Forces 31: 265-273.

NETTLER, G. (1978) Explaining Crime. New York: McGraw-Hill.

NEUMAN, W. L. (1977) "Corporate influence on the Federal Trade Commission: the trade practice conferences." Presented at the annual meetings of the American Sociological Association, Chicago, September.

NIEBUHR, R. (1960) Moral Man and Immoral Society. New York: Scribner's. (originally pubiished in 1932)

NONET, P. (1976) "For jurisprudential sociology." Law and Society Review 10: 525-545.

OTTEN, A. (1975) "Guns do kill people," Wall Street Journal (Nov. 13): 18.

PACKER, H. L. (1968) The Limits of Criminal Sanction. Stanford, CA: Stanford University Press.

PARSONS, T. (1937) The Structure of Social Action. New York: Free Press.

—— (1951) The Social System, New York: Free Press.

PASSELL, P. (1975) "The deterrent effect of the death penalty: a statistical test."
Stanford Law Review 28: 61-80.

——— and J. B. TAYLOR (1977) "The deterrent effect of capital punishment;
another view." The American Economic Review 67: 445-451.

PECK, D. G. (1977) "Social influence, perception of certainty, and perception of
celerity in deterring adolescent marijuana use." (unpublished)

PEPINSKY, H. E. (1978) "Communist anarchism as an alternative to the rule of
criminal law." Contemporary Crises 2(July): 315-334.

PHILLIPS, W. (1964) "Canadian Combines Policy—The Matter of Mergers."
Canadian Bar Review 42(March): 88-99.

PLATT, A. M. (1969) The Child Savers: The Intervention of Delinquency. Chicago:
University of Chicago Press.

PODGORECKI, A. (1973) "Public opinion on law," pp. 65-100 in A. Podgorecki,
W. Kaupen, J. Van Houtte, P. Vinke, and B. Kutchinsky (eds.) Knowledge and
Opinion about Law. South Hackensack, NJ: Fred B. Rothman.

PONTELL, H. N. (1978) "Deterrence: theory versus practice." Criminology 16:
3-22.

POUND, R. (1959) Jurisprudence (5 vols.) St. Paul, MN: West.

QUINNEY, R. (1969) Crime and Justice in Society. Boston: Little, Brown.

——— (1974) Critique of Legal Order: Crime Control in Capitalist Society. Boston:
Little, Brown.

——— (1977) Class, State, and Crime: On the Theory and Practice of Criminal
Justice. Boston: Little, Brown.

QUINTON, A. M. (1954) "On punishment." Analysis 14: 512-517.

RAPOPORT, A. (1974) Conflict in Man-Made Environment. New York: Penguin.

RASHDALL, H. (1924) Theory of Good and Evil. Oxford: Clarendon.

REID, S. T. (1979) Crime and Criminology. New York: Holt, Rinehart & Winston.

REITZE, A. W., Jr. and G. L. REITZE (1976) "Buccaneering: kepone and Allied
Chemical/Life Science Products Co." Environment (March): 2-5.

RIDGEWAY, J. (1970) The Politics of Ecology. New York: E. P. Dutton.

ROSE, A. (1967) The Power Structure: Political Process in America. New York:
Oxford University Press.

ROSENBAUM, W. A. (1977) The Politics of Environmental Concern. New York:
Praeger.

ROSENBERG, N. (1972) Technology and American Economic Growth. White
Plains, NY: M. E. Sharpe.

SAPIR, E. (1931) "Communication." Encyclopaedia of the Social Sciences 4:
78-80.

——— (1933) "Language." Encyclopaedia of the Social Sciences 9: 155-169.

SAVITZ, L. D. (1958) "A study of capital punishment." Journal of Criminal Law,
Criminology and Police Science 49: 338-341.

SCHUESSLER, K. F. (1952) "The deterrent influence of the death penalty." Annals
of the American Academy of Political and Social Science 284: 54-62.

SCHWARTZ, R. D. and J. C. MILLER (1964) "Legal revolution and societal complexity." American Journal of Sociology 70(September): 159-169.

SEITZ, S. (1978) Bureaucracy, Policy, and the Public. St. Louis, MO: C. V. Mosby.

SELLIN, T. (1967) "Homicides in retentionist and abolitionist states," pp. 135-138
in T. Sellin (ed.) Capital Punishment. New York: Harper & Row.

SELZNICK, P. (1966) The TVA and the Grass Roots. New York: Harper.
—— (1968) "The Sociology of Law." International Encyclopedia of the Social Sciences 9: 50-59.
SILBERMAN, M. (1976) "Toward a theory of criminal deterrence." American Sociological Review 41: 442-461.
SIMPSON, G. (1963) Emile Durkheim. New York: Thomas Y. Crowell.
SKOLNICK, J. H. (1965) "The sociology of law in America: overview and trends." Social Problems (special summer supplement): 4-39.
SNIDER, D. L. (1977) "Does the legal system reflect the power structure: a test of conflict theory." Ph.D. dissertation, University of Toronto.
—— (1978) "Corporate Crime in Canada: A Preliminary Report." Canadian Journal of Criminology 20(April): 142-169.
SNOW, C. P. (1962) Science and Government. New York: Mentor.
STANBURY, W. T. (1975) "Canadian attitudes toward competition policy: the dominance of business interests." Presented at the Seminar of the Canadian Consumer Research Council, February. (unpublished)
—— (1977) Business Interests and the Reform of Canadian Competition Policy, 1971-1975. Toronto: Carswell.
STONE, C. D. (1977) "A slap on the wrist for the kepone mob." Business and Society Review 22 (Summer): 4-11.
SULLIVAN, D. S. and L. TIFFT (1977) "Anarchy: a non-sequitur of criminology—a new vision of justice and social order without the state." Presented at the annual meetings of American Society of Criminology, Atlanta, November.
SUMNER, W. G. (1906) Folkways: A Study of the Sociological Importance of Usages, Manners, Customs, Mores, and Morals. Boston: Ginn.
SUTHERLAND, E. H. (1947) Principles of Criminology. Philadelphia, PA: Lippincott.
—— and D.R. CRESSEY (1970, 1978) Criminology. Philadelphia, PA: Lippincott.
SYKES, G. M. (1978) Criminology. New York: Harcourt, Brace Jovanovich.
TAPPAN, P. W. (1969) Court for Wayward Girls. Montclair, NJ: Patterson Smith.
TAYLOR, I., P. WALTON, and J. YOUNG (1973) The New Criminology. London: Routledge and Kegan Paul.
TAYLOR, P. A. (1972) An Introduction to Statistical Methods. Itasca, IL: F. E. Peacock.
TEEVAN, J. J. Jr. (1975) "Perceptions of punishment: current research," pp. 146-154 in R. L. Henshel and R. A. Silberman (eds.) Perception in Criminology. New York: Columbia University Press.
—— (1976a) "Subjective perception of deterrence (continued)." Journal of Research in Crime and Delinquency 13: 155-164.
—— (1976b) "Deterrent effects of punishment: subjective measures continued." Canadian Journal of Criminology and Corrections 18: 152-160.
—— (1977) "Deterrent effects of punishment for breaking and entering and theft." Canadian Journal of Criminology and Corrections 19: 121-149.
THOMAS, C. W. (1977) The effect of legal sanctions on juvenile delinquency: a comparison of the labeling and deterrence perspectives. Bowling Green State University. (unpublished)
THOMPSON, E. P. (1975) Whigs and Hunters: The Origin of the Black Act. New York: Pantheon.
TIRYAKIAN, E. A. (1962) Sociologism and Existentialism. Englewood Cliffs, NJ: Prentice-Hall.

TITTLE, C. R. (1969) "Crime rates and legal sanctions." Social Problems 16: 409-423.
—— (1977) "Sanction fear and the maintenance of social order." Social Forces 55: 579-596.
—— (1978) "Comment on 'deterrence: theory versus practice.'" Criminology 16: 31-35.
—— and C. H. LOGAN (1973) "Sanctions and deviance: evidence and remaining questions." Law and Society Review 7: 371-392.
TURK, A. T. (1969) Criminality and Legal Order. Chicago: Rand McNally.
—— (1974) "Political Criminality: Implications for Social Change." ET AL: Crime and Law in a Changing Society 3, 3.
—— (1976) "Law as a weapon in social conflict." Social Problems 23 (February): 276-291.
TURNER, J. S. (1970) The Chemical Feast. New York: Grossman.
UNGAR, R. M. (1976) Law in Modern Society. New York: Free Press.
VAN DEN HAAG, E. (1975) Punishing Criminals. New York: Basic Books.
VOLD, G. B. (1958) Theoretical Criminology. New York: Oxford University Press.
VON HIRSCH, A. (1975) Doing Justice: The Choice of Punishments. New York: Hill and Wang.
WALDO, G. P. and T. G. CHIRICOS (1972) "Perceived penal sanctions and self-reported criminality: a neglected approach to deterrence research." Social Problems 19: 522-540.
WALKER, N. (1964) "Morality and the criminal law." Howard Journal 11(3): 209-219.
—— (1967) "Evidence before the Royal Commission on the Panel System. (unpublished manuscript)
—— and M. ARGYLE (1964) "Does the law affect moral judgments? British Journal of Criminology 4(October): 570-581.
WEBER, M. (1958) From Max Weber [ed.] (H. H. Gerth and C. W. Mills, trans). New York: Galaxy.
—— (1964) The Theory of Social and Economic Organization (T. Parsons, ed.) New York: Free Press.
—— (1968) Economy and Society. New York: Bedminster.
WELDON, J. C. (1966) "Consolidations in Canadian Industry, 1900-1948," pp. 228-279 in G. Skeoch (ed.) Restrictive Trade Practices in Canada. Toronto: McClelland and Stewart.
WENNER, L. M. (1972) "Enforcement of water pollution control laws in the United States." Ph.D. dissertation, University of Wisconsin—Madison.
—— (1974) "Federal water pollution control statutes in theory and practice." Environmental Law (Winter): 251-293.
WIGMORE, J. H. (1926) "Juvenile Court vs. Criminal Court," Illinois Law Review 21: 375-377.
WILSON, J. Q. (1975) Thinking about Crime. New York: Basic Books.
WIMBERLEY, H. (1973) "Legal evolution: one further step." American Journal of Sociology 79 (July): 78-83.
ZEITLIN, I. M. (1968) Ideology and the Development of Sociological Theory. Englewood Cliffs, NJ: Prentice-Hall.
ZIMRING, F. and G. HAWKINS (1971) "The legal threat as an instrument of social change." Journal of Social Issues 27(2): 33-48.
ZWICK, D. R. and M. BENSTOCK (1971) Water Wasteland. New York: Grossman.

ABOUT THE AUTHORS

PAUL J. BRANTINGHAM is Associate Professor of Criminology and Chairman of the Graduate Program in Criminology at Simon Fraser University. He is the co-author of *Juvenile Justice Philosophy* and is currently working on a book entitled, *Patterns in Crime*. His research interests include law, environmental criminology, and history of crime. He is a member of the state bar of California.

JACK M. KRESS is a graduate of Columbia Law School and Cambridge University, England. Since 1973, Professor Kress has been teaching at the Graduate School of Criminal Justice at the State University of New York at Albany. From 1969 to 1973, he was an Assistant District Attorney to Frank S. Hogan in New York County. He has published nine books and monographs on the topics of law, the courts and sentencing, and he has served as a criminal justice consultant to numerous organizations including the National Judicial College, the United Nations Social Defense Research Institute, the Police Foundation, and the Vera Institute of Justice. Professor Kress developed and implemented the original sentencing guidelines systems in Denver, Chicago, Newark, and Phoenix, and is collaborating with the judiciary in many other states and local jurisdictions in developing similar systems as aids to local trial court judges.

RONALD L. AKERS is Professor and Chairman of the Department of Sociology at the University of Iowa. He has research interests in criminology, sociology of law, and deviance. He is author of *Deviant Behavior: A Social Learning Approach* and coeditor of *Law and Control in Society, Crime Prevention and Social Control,* and *Crime, Law, and Sanctions*.

LINDA S. ANDERSON is Assistant Professor of Sociology at Mankato State University. Her research interests include empirical tests of deterrence and social control theory.

RICHARD A. BALL is Professor of Sociology at West Virginia University. His current interests include criminological theory, rural delinquency research, and studies in deviance. Recent work includes articles on dialectical theory, (*Social Forces*), general systems theory (*The American Sociologist*), Mexican medicine hucksters (*Sociology of Work and Occupations*), and evaluation research (*Sociological Focus*).

MARSHALL B. CLINARD is Professor of Sociology at the University of Wisconsin—Madison. He is author of a number of books, including *Sociology of Deviant Behavior* and his latest *Cities with Little Crime: The Case of Switzerland,* and co-author of *Crime in Developing Countries* and *Criminal Behavior Systems: A Typology*. He received the Edwin H. Sutherland award in 1971 and was named a Fellow of the American Society of Criminology in 1977.

WILLIAM JEFFREY, Jr. is Professor of Law at the University of Cincinnati. His research and teaching interests lie in the fields of property law, comparative law, sociology of law, Soviet legal institutions, and American legal history. His translation of Durkheim's "Two Laws of Penal Evolution" appeared in 1969, and an edition of the "Letters of Brutus" was published in 1971.

MARVIN D. KROHN is Assistant Professor of Sociology at the University of Iowa. His research interests include cross-national comparisons of crime, adolescent substance use, and legal socialization. He recently coedited a volume entitled, *Crime, Law, and Sanctions.*

LONN LANZA-KADUCE has a law degree from the University of Iowa where he is currently a Ph.D. candidate in the Department of Sociology. His research interests include sociology of law, criminology and deviance, and he is presently working with a research project evaluating the effectiveness of prison programs.

MARCIA RADOSEVICH is a Ph.D. candidate in the Department of Sociology at the University of Iowa. Her research interests include legal socialization, adolescent substance abuse, and female criminality.

STEVEN THOMAS SEITZ is Assistant Professor in the Department of Political Science at the University of Illinois-Urbana/Champaign. His research interests include policy formation, implementation, and evaluation, with special emphasis on criminal justice policy. He is the author of *Bureaucracy, Policy, and the Public,* several articles, and currently is completing *Models of the Policy Process.*

D. LAUREEN SNIDER is an Assistant Professor of Sociology at Queen's University in Kingston, Ontario, Canada. She has published two recent articles on corporate crime in Canada. Her current research interests center around the concept of "reform" in the capitalist state as exemplified by legal aid legislation and delivery systems. She recently completed an evalution of a rural legal aid program for the Department of Justice, Ottawa.

AUSTIN T. TURK is Professor of Sociology and Criminology in the Department of Sociology and Centre of Criminology at the University of Toronto. His research interests include the sociology of law, deviance, and social control, and theoretical criminology. His most recent book is *Political Criminality and Political Policing* (Dubuque, Iowa: William C. Brown, in press).

PETER C. YEAGER is Assistant Professor of Sociology at Yale University. He was senior research assistant on a research project on corporate crime directed by Marshall B. Clinard. His dissertation concerned the development of the environmental regulation of corporations, and his current research interests include the nature and control of corporate and professional behavior.